The Changing Face of Denominationalism

Edited by Kyle Pope

Truth Publications / CEIbooks
220 S. Marion St., Athens, AL 35611
855.492.6657 | sales@ceibooks.com

© **Guardian of Truth Foundation 2016.** All rights reserved. No part of this book may be reproduced in any form without written permission from the publisher. Printed in the United States of America.

ISBN 10: 1-58427-4352
ISBN 13: 978-1-58427-4353

Truth Publications / CEIbooks
220 S. Marion St., Athens, AL 35611
855.492.6657 | sales@ceibooks.com

Table of Contents

Preface 5

It's a Different World 7

The "Non-Denominational" Denomination 15

The "Church of Christ" Denomination 21

The "Mega-Church" Mentality—What Can the Church Do for Me? 27

"Let Your Women *Not* Be Silent in the Churches" 31

The Moral Fog of Modern Religion 37

"Nones" and "Dones"—The Rise of Non-Religious Religion 43

From *Sola Scriptura* to *Nulla Scriptura* 47

Empty Pews and Geographical Shifts: 53

Is an Impending Catholic – Protestant Convergence Coming? 59

"No One Comes to the Father Except through *Whom*?" 65

Conservative Thinking within the Denominational World 69

Is It Still Possible to be Simply Christians? 75

Appendix: Faith in Faith vs. Faith in God 83

Preface

In May of 2015 brother Mike Willis asked me if I would be interested in editing an issue of *Truth Magazine* on "The Changing Face of Denominationalsim" considering modern developments within the religious world. After accepting his offer, I submitted a proposal to him of topics and possible authors. Given that these developments dramatically influence how members of the church work to convert those in religious error, brother Willis suggested that we expand the study to present this topic in two issues of the magazine, then compile it into a workbook for brethren. The following study is the product of this effort.

On the pages that follow you will find thirteen studies compiled by twelve gospel preachers examining some of the issues and developments that are changing the denominational environment of our time. You will also find an excellent article written by brother Willis that we have included as an appendix addressing the mindset that has contributed to these changes. My thanks goes out to the men who contributed so generously of their time and excellent study to make this project a reality. We should note, this is not a study focusing on the background and specific beliefs of major denominations. There are many good studies that accomplish this purpose and might serve as good preparation for this study. The fact is our world has seen a blurring of many of these lines of distinction as the denominational world has splintered further into greater division and apostasy. The aim of this study is to alert, inform, and prepare Christians to confront shifting dynamics they may encounter with friends, family, and those whom they seek to influence. May the Lord bless its use to this end for His ultimate glory.

Kyle Pope 2015

kmpope@att.net

Origen
(184-253 AD)

"Where there are sins, there is plurality, there are schisms, there are heresies, there is dissension; but where there is virtue, there is singularity, there is unity, from which all who believed were 'one heart and one soul' (Acts 4:32). To put it more clearly, the beginning of all evils is plurality, but the beginning of good is in limiting oneself and in singularity withdrawing from the popular turmoil. As for example, if we all are to be saved, in unity we must be made perfect 'in the same mind and in the same judgment' (1 Cor, 1:10), and we must be 'one body and one spirit' (Eph. 4:4)."

Homily on Ezekiel, 9.2, Pope

It's a Different World

By Kyle Pope

Lesson 1

When I first began preaching in the late 1980s, I picked up a book at a used bookstore entitled *Handbook of Denominations,* by Frank Mead. It was a helpful book that listed the major religious bodies in the United States at the time of its publication, with brief descriptions of their beliefs and history. While I didn't like that the book counted churches of Christ within its listing of "denominations," I appreciated that it explained under its entry, "They do not think of themselves as being denominational but 'rather desire to be as the church of the first century.'"[1] By my count the book listed 223 distinct groups among those who claimed a belief in Jesus.

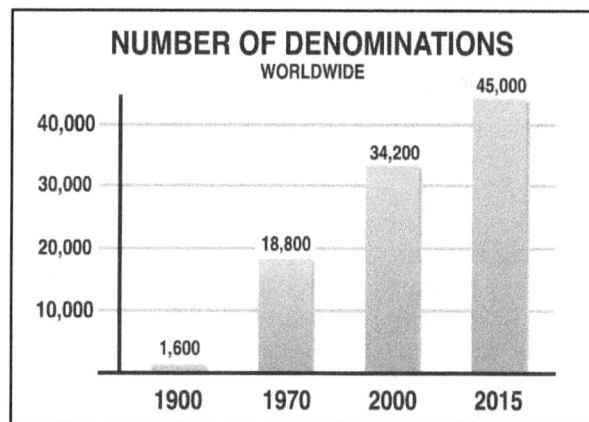

What I didn't realize at the time was that the book, written in 1951 (and based on statistics going back as far as 1936), was describing conditions decades out of date by the time I purchased it. According to the Center for the Study of Global Christianity at Gordon-Criswell Theological Seminary, by 1970 worldwide there were 18,800 denominations, and by the year 2000 that number had risen to 34,200.[2] While the book I purchased was only looking at groups in the United States, and the statistics from Gordon-Criswell reflect global numbers, the fact is that the religious picture of the world around us has become more and more divided and confused. As I write, according to estimates from that same study, the number has now grown to 45,000!

The chaos of an apostate world does not change the singular nature of the Lord's church. When the Lord's church was first established there was **"one body"** (Eph. 4:4), and those who abide in the word of Christ continue as disciples of Christ (John 8:31) and members of that **"one body in Christ, and individually members of one another"** (Rom. 12:5). It is important, however, for Christians in the twenty-first century to understand the changes that have affected the religious world around us in order to effectively call people out of error and confusion.

What Has Changed?

Increasingly among those who consider themselves "Christians," more and more of these groups reject beliefs as fundamental as a belief in the inspiration of Scripture, the reality of hell as a punishment for sin, or even Christ as the sole author of salvation. In 1980 Mike Willis wrote an article in *Truth Magazine* entitled "Changes in Denominationalism." Willis observed at that time a growing ecumenical attitude that taught sincerity as the sole criterion for salvation and a willingness to condemn few doctrines or practices as sinful.[3] In the 35 years since Willis wrote, the religious world has not only advanced many of these same attitudes, but it has expanded to adopt practices and teachings far different from the traditional denominational views of the nineteenth and early twentieth centuries. Notable among these changes are some of the following developments.

Changing Definitions of Denominationalism

Membership in many major denominations has declined in recent years. According to the US

---

[1] Mead, Frank S. *Handbook of Denominations in the United States.* New York, Abingdon Press, 1951, 60.
[2] Johnson, Todd M., Gina A. Zurlo, Albert W. Hickman, and Peter F. Crossing. "Christianity 2015: Religious Diversity and Personal Contact." *International Bulletin of Missionary Research.* 39.1 (Jan. 2015) 28-29.
[3] Willis, Mike. "Changes in Denominationalism." *Truth Magazine* 24.49 (Dec. 11, 1980) 787-789.

Declines In Major Denominations

	1990	2008
Methodist	14,174,000	11,336,000
Lutheran	9,110,000	8,674,000
Presbyterian	4,985,000	4,723,000
Episcopalian	3,043,000	2,405,000

Census Bureau, from 1990-2008 membership in Methodist, Lutheran, Presbyterian, and Episcopalian churches all declined (61).[4] In many cases "non-denominational" denominations have arisen from those who have left their former denominational allegiance. Ironically these "non-denominational" churches do not oppose denominational teachings or practices, but simply seek organizational independence. Some of these have become "mini-denominations," training their own preachers, founding their own institutions, and establishing satellite churches following their own model. These changes blur and confuse what is even meant by using the term *denomination* in reference to religious sects. Paul's command to be **"perfectly joined together in the same mind and in the same judgment"** (1 Cor. 1:10) is increasingly ignored as an ideal that is unattainable.

These changing definitions have even affected churches of Christ. Congregations that once opposed denominationalism, now embrace identification of themselves as members of the "Church of Christ" denomination. Over fifty years ago Ed Harrell warned in 1962, "The time may not be far distant when considerable numbers of Churches of Christ will be proud of their denominational status" (27).[5] Sadly, that time has now come! Large congregations often participate in co-operative projects with denominations without reservation. Paul's call to **"note those who cause divisions and offenses, contrary to the doctrine which you learned, and avoid them"** (Rom. 16:17) is now seen as *old-fashioned* and *narrow-minded* thinking.

Finally, dissatisfaction with the current state of the religious world has led to rising numbers of people who have rejected organized religion altogether. These people, whom some have called "nones" (from the fact that they claim no affiliation) or "dones" (in that they have rejected former affiliations), adopt concepts of spirituality that are individual in nature or composed of loose associations with those of similar thought. Author Thom Schultz explains that they have tired of the "plop, pray, and pay" routine, and now are simply "done."[6] All of these changes affect where we can even begin in seeking to bring those outside of

> These changing definitions have even affected churches of Christ. Congregations that once opposed denominationalism, now embrace identification of themselves as members of the "Church of Christ" denomination.

[4] "Table 75. Self-Described Religious Identification of Adult Population: 1990, 2001, and 2008." *Statistical Abstract of the United States: 2012.* Ed. U.S. Census Bureau. Washington, D.C.: U.S. Census Bureau, 2012.

[5] Harrell, David Edwin Jr. *The Emergence of the Church of Christ Denomination.* Athens AL: CEI Pub. Co., 1972.
[6] Schultz, Thom. "The Rise of the Dones." *Holysoup.com*

> There was a time when we shared many things in common with denominationalists with regard to what was considered right and wrong. Sadly, that is no longer the case.

Christ into sound faith. This is especially true when we encounter…

Changing Standards of Right and Wrong

There was a time when (in spite of our differences with denominationalists over doctrines of salvation and the work and worship of the church) we shared many things in common with regard to what was considered right and wrong. Sadly, that is no longer the case. We now face dramatic differences regarding…

Attitudes toward the Bible

Sound teaching has long forced us to oppose the Catholic and Orthodox positions that Scripture and "Sacred Tradition" hold equal value in establishing authority for doctrine and practice. We have shared in common with Protestants an affirmation that the "Scriptures alone" (*sola scriptura*) are the standard of authority. Jesus taught that His disciples must reject religious tradition that is contrary to God's word (Matt. 15:3-9). Paul taught that Scripture can make one **"complete, thoroughly equipped for every good work"** (2 Tim. 3:16-17). Yet, as the nineteenth century introduced critical scholarly theories that imagined evolutionary concepts of the man-made formation of Scripture, those who once trusted in the authority of the Bible began to place their trust in the wisdom and learning of man rather than the revelation of God. On the other extreme, the rise of charismatic movements within traditional denominations alongside Pentecostal denominations claiming to possess miraculous spiritual gifts has led to a different type of rejection of biblical authority. If people believe that the Holy Spirit is personally directing them, they will feel little need to study Scripture. So like the Catholics, they actually trust in a second standard of authority: the Bible and their own personal feelings (which they attribute to the Holy Spirit). Paul taught that any type of perceived additional revelation that runs contrary to Scripture must be rejected (cf. Gal. 1:8-9). With this confused view of the Bible it is little wonder that many pulpits now use Scripture as mere "filler" between emotional stories and humorous anecdotes.

Attitudes toward Gender Roles

Changes within a culture inevitably bring changes in religious thinking. As women's roles have expanded in the workplace and the political arena much of the religious world now rejects biblical restrictions on women's roles within the church. The popularity of denominational teachers such as Beth Moore and others has led many who once followed biblical patterns to ignore what the Bible teaches on women's roles. Clearly, the Bible teaches women to teach other women (Titus 2:3-4), children (2 Tim. 1:5), and in situations outside of the church assembly they may discuss spiritual matters with men (cf. Acts 18:26). Yet, even in these situations a Christian woman is to maintain a quiet and submissive disposition (1 Tim. 2:12-14). It is clear, however, with the exception of confession of Christ and singing, that in the assembly of the church a woman is to be silent (1

[online] *http://holysoup.com/2014/11/12/the-rise-of-the-dones/*.

Cor. 14:34-35). Now, in spite of this, even within sound congregations we are beginning to see struggles to uphold biblical teaching in the face of a culture highly resistant to any gender restrictions.

Attitudes Toward Morality

Increasingly people who claim religious convictions accept moral values that dramatically conflict with biblical teaching. A February 2015 PBS story reported that there are presently over 130 churches in the US that meet in bars, with beer served while services are conducted.[7] Preacher Bryan Berghoef has authored a book entitled *Pub Theology* advocating religious discussions over shared alcoholic drinks as a legitimate venue for religious investigation.[8] Didn't Paul rebuke the Corinthians for bringing social meals into the church assembly (1 Cor. 11:22)? Didn't Peter teach that "drinking parties" were something one leaves behind when becoming a Christian (1 Pet. 4:3)? How can we imagine these things are acceptable before God?

This is also true in matters of sexual morality. Retired Anglican Priest, Robert Brow argues, "The Bible does not forbid premarital sex. There is no passage of the Bible that references premarital sex as a sin against God."[9] Does Scripture not speak of it as "a disgraceful thing" and something "which ought not be done" (Gen. 34:7)? Unfortunately, this is not a new tendency. Long ago denominationalists embraced unscriptural attitudes toward modesty, sex outside of marriage, divorce, and they are increasingly tolerant of homosexuality. None of these changing views of human beings changes anything within the word of God! The Holy Spirit teaches, "Neither fornicators, nor idolaters, nor adulterers, nor homosexuals, nor sodomites," will inherit the kingdom of God (1 Cor. 6:9).

Robert C. Brow

Made-to-Order Religion

Perhaps one of the greatest changes in attitude is seen in a different view of the very purpose of faith. There is little talk in the modern world about *pleasing God*. It is assumed that if something pleases us, it *must* please God. Israel was warned in the Law not to do as they ended up doing during the time of the Judges—doing whatever each thought was "right in his own eyes" (Deut. 12:8; Judg. 17:6; 21:25). In our world churches will actually survey communities to learn what people are looking for in the churches that are within their neighborhoods.[10]

This "as you like it" religion has had a profound impact on the religious world. Churches have become market-driven supercenters offering everything modern man imagines. This might include anything from knitting classes and exercise rooms, to financial counseling, daycare, and retreats to exotic locations. This thinking has changed expectations of the nature of religion. It is no longer a matter of worship aimed at pleasing God. The focus is now on what a church can do for us.

---

[7] Severson, Lucky. "Churches in Pubs." *Religion & Ethics Newsweekly: PBS.org* (Feb. 20, 2015) [online] *http://www.pbs.org/wnet/religionandethics/2015/02/20/february-20-2015-churches-pubs/25265/*.

[8] Berghoef, Bryan. *Pub Theology: Beer, Conversation, and God*. Eugene, OR: Wipf and Stock Pub., 2012.

[9] Brow, Robert. "Premarital Sex is Not a Sin Against God." *123HelpMe.com*. [online]. *http://www.123HelpMe.com/view.asp?id=163282*.

[10] Cimino, Richard and Don Lattin. "Choosing My Religion." *American Demographics* (April 1999), 60-65.

Many churches now operate coffee shops inside their place of meeting.

History has revealed the dangerous consequences of this type of approach. Since the time of the Protestant Reformation, the Roman Catholic Church was criticized for assimilating pagan concepts into religious practice in order to win converts. John Calvin criticized the Catholic Church for merging myths associated with pagan gods into legends about "saints." In his work *A Treatise on Relics* he accused them of "substituting the agency of the Christian saint, the hero of their tale, for that of the Pagan deity, to whom it had originally been ascribed" (8). As the Bible teaches it there are no special and isolated Christians whom the church is authorized to canonize as "saints." As the Bible teaches it, all Christians are "saints," i.e. *those set apart* unto God (1 Cor. 1:2). Even so, this practice of venerating "saints" and relics (which is drawn out of pagan religion) has continued throughout history. William Madsen, in his book *The Virgin's Children: Life in an Aztec Village Today,* addresses this as it was seen in Mexico following the Spanish conquest of the Aztecs. He explains:

> Catholic saints gradually assumed most of the functions of Aztec gods. Before the Conquest each Aztec village had an idol of a patron god who protected the pueblo. Indians adorned the village idol with robes and jewels and gave it offerings. After the Conquest each town adopted a patron saint, who received clothing and offerings from the villagers in return for providing them with the necessities of life (Chapter 2: Conquest and Conversion).[11]

Jesus taught that acts of worship not authorized by the word of God are "vain" or useless (Matt. 15:9). Modern market-driven churches may not venerate relics and images, but they are doing exactly the same thing. They unashamedly focus on what potential converts want and shape their practice after these desires. This thinking has subtly worked its way into our own mindset, as we place less and less emphasis on what God wants and more on our own feelings and desires. May it be in us, as the Hebrew writer prayed, that God might make us "complete in every good work to do His will, working in you what is well pleasing in His sight" (Heb. 13:21).

Opportunities in the Midst of Chaos

We should not end such a study without recognizing that in the midst of the increasing turmoil and confusion of the world around us, there are also important opportunities that such changes present. The growing ecumenical attitude of our world, and potential convergence of factions once separated by competing doctrines reflects a desire (on some level) to achieve our Lord's prayer that all who believe in Him "may be one" (John 17:11, 21). Our task must be to help such souls see that true unity is not accomplished by superficially coming together accommodating everything man might imagine to be "right in his own eyes" (Deut. 12:8). It is accomplished in standing together on the sound teachings of God's word! Every time that a soul grows disillusioned with the false hope of denominationalism, an opportunity arises to help that soul understand "the way of God more accurately" (Acts 18:26). In spite of the negative attitudes and improper thinking that exists, there

---

[11] Madsen, William. *The Virgin's Children: Life in an Aztec Village Today.* Austin: University of Texas Press, 1960.

are, nevertheless, people in error with good attitudes just waiting to learn the truth. These are souls "not far from the kingdom of God" (Mark 12:34). May God help us to seek them, find them, and share with them the glorious riches of the truth of God's word!

KYLE POPE

Study Questions

1. According to research done by Gordon-Criswell how many denominations existed worldwide in these years?

    1900: _____ 1970: _____

    2000: _____ 2015: _____

    How does this comare to what is taught in Ephesians 4:4? _____
    _____
    _____

2. According to US Census numbers, list four major denominations that have shown declines in membership from 1990-2008:

    1) _____ 2) _____

    3) _____ 4) _____

    What are some factors that explain some of these declines? _____
    _____
    _____

3. What does 1 Corinthians 1:10 teach that runs counter to the concept of denominationalism? _____
    _____
    _____

4. Why is it wrong for churches of Christ to begin to identify themselves as part of the "Church of Christ" denomination? _____
    _____
    _____

    Does Romans 16:17 teach anything about this question? _____
    _____
    _____

5. What might lead some to feel like religion is just a "plop, pray, and pay" routine? _____
    _____
    _____

    How can we help Christians with whom we worship avoid coming to feel this way about their relationship to the church? _____
    _____

6. What are two ways that denominationalists have come to imagine that there are two standards that govern what the church does? _____
    _____
    _____

    What does 2 Timothy 3:16-17 teach about this? _____
    _____
    _____

7. In what three areas can we identify changing attitudes in the religious world toward right and wrong?
   1) _____ 2) _____
   3) _____

   Have you seen examples of this? _____
   _____
   _____

8. What did Mosaic Law forbid that the Israelites did during the time of the Judges (Deut. 12:8; Judg. 17:6; 21:25)? _____
   _____

   How does this relate to religion in today's world? _____
   _____
   _____

Lesson 2

The "Non-Denominational" Denomination

By Shawn Chancellor

> If viewed as a whole, the nondenominational churches form the second largest branch of Protestant denominations in the United States.

Over the past several decades there has been a growing dissatisfaction with the status quo among religious people. Among the denominations, this dissatisfaction has resulted in a multitude of people leaving and forming new groups often referred to as nondenominational churches. Like the churches of Christ, who have used that term to describe themselves, these churches have laid aside any formal allegiance to creed or convention, along with many of the traditions that have defined the denominations since their inception.

According to a recent survey published by Pew Research Center, if viewed as a whole, the nondenominational churches form the second largest branch of Protestant denominations in the United Sates. The Baptist churches represent 15.4% of the total population of the country, the nondenominational churches 6.2% and the Methodist churches 4.2% and this trend is accelerating. In the period between 2007 and 2014 only the nondenominational churches showed any significant growth, rising 1.7% while the Baptist churches declined 1.8% and the Methodist 2%.[1]

This trend seems to be an outgrowth of the evangelical movement, which is highly focused on the emotional experience of worshipping God and emphasizes the concept of a personal relationship with Jesus Christ. In order to further these goals, the evangelicals moved away from discussions about the need for baptism, the significance of the Lord's Supper, the role of women in public worship, etc. By intentionally avoiding issues that might be considered divisive, these churches lack the restrictive feel that many felt had come to define the traditional denominations. With an emphasis on acceptance and an intensely emotional worship

---

[1] "America's Changing Religious Landscape," Appendix B (May 12, 2015 http://www.pewforum.org/2015/05/12/appendix-b-classification-of-protestant-denominations/. It is important to note that for the purposes of this survey all groups of a similar tradition were viewed as a whole, for example the Southern Baptist Convention, American Baptist Churches USA, National Baptist Convention, etc. were grouped together under the heading "Baptist." The Nondenominational churches were viewed in similar fashion combining evangelical, charismatic, fundamentalist, etc.

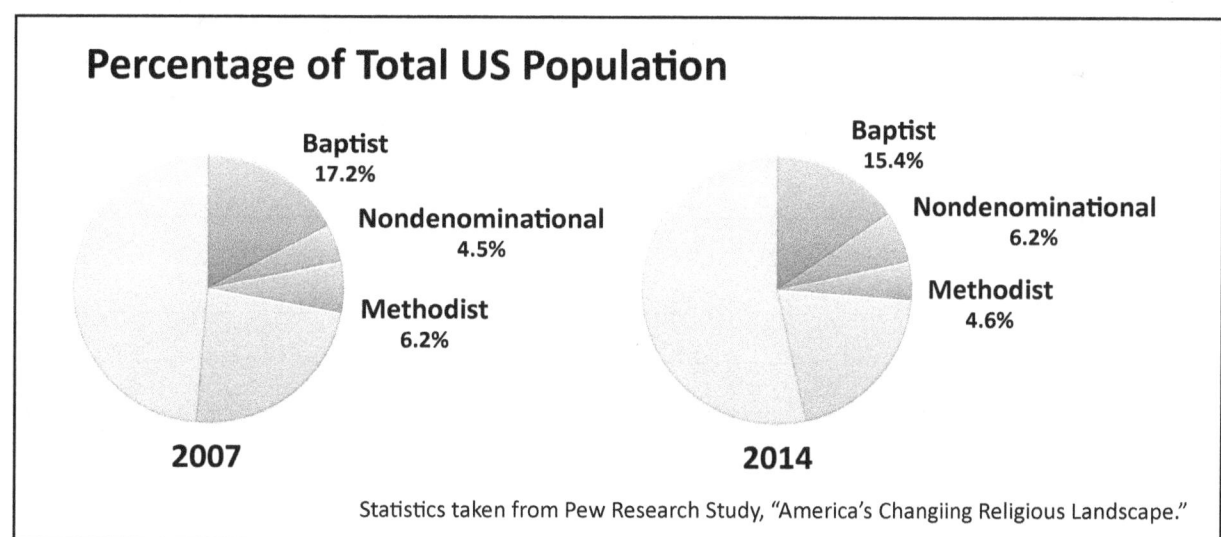

Statistics taken from Pew Research Study, "America's Changiing Religious Landscape."

> Doctrinally many of these churches refelect a Baptist background mixed with a heavy charismatic influence.

service, these churches have found a growing niche in today's rapidly evolving millennial driven culture. Many offer multiple services with their own peculiar flavor, from traditional Protestant style worship services to more "contemporary" worship with elements intentionally designed to appeal to the young.

Their localized church government allows for rapid and seemingly limitless adaptation. Much of this growth should be attributed to the commercialized approach taken by many, especially the larger nondenominational churches. While some of these churches seem like mirror images of the denomination from which they departed, many present unique blends of Baptist, Pentecostal, and prosperity theology. A greater emphasis is placed on the worship experience than the doctrine presented. A typical Sunday worship program will include professionally produced, focus-grouped, "music services," large format video boards projecting professional quality presentations from well-known personalities, and one new trend is "sermons illustrated by movies scenes" in which clips from popular movies are played in order to illustrate the sermon all in the name of reaching and engaging new people.

Doctrinally many of these churches reflect a Baptist background mixed with a heavy charismatic influence (26% of congregations employ tongue speaking and 27% utilize prophecy).[2] While the majority of members state that the sermons they hear are biblically centered, one has only to visit a sampling of websites to find that, in reality, the trend is toward an ecumenical, social gospel, which is carefully marketed to a group that has become dissatisfied with the traditional denominations. While the fact of God's offer of salvation is a frequent topic, a deep discussion on the means of that salvation will be difficult to find. Instead the cross becomes a means to speak about more "practical" things such as satisfaction in the workplace while steering away from clear denunciation of any sinful activity or a need for true repentance. The carefully choreographed worship experience distracts one from the lack of substantive preaching and the failure to connect the Bible story to the life of the worshiper.

This ecumenical mentality is of course in direct conflict with the approach of the church in the first century. In Paul's two letters to Timothy, we see clear instruction to teach on many of the issues deemed too divisive among the nondenominational churches, such as gender roles, qualifications of leaders, and regulations for benevolent work. Furthermore, in 1 Timothy 4 he admonishes Timothy to deal directly with issues that would divide brethren going so far as to say that **"in pointing out these things to the brethren, you will be a good servant of Christ Jesus"** (v. 6, NASB).

It is essential that we recognize the connection between the doctrine of the Gospel and the practice of the church. In 1 Timothy 3:15 Paul says, "I write so that you will know how one ought to conduct himself in the household of God, which is the church of the living God, the pillar and support of truth." This drawing together of faith and practice continues throughout both letters in such a manner that it is often difficult to distinguish between the two. For example, in 1 Timothy 4:1-5, he warns of

---

2 "Nondenominational Congregations Today" (*http://www.hartfordinstitute.org/cong/nondenom_FACT.html#worship*).

NOTES

the coming practice of forbidding marriage and advocating abstinence from certain foods, and in v. 6 he tells Timothy that in pointing out the error of these practices he will be **"constantly nourished on the words of the faith and of the sound doctrine...."** One cannot innovate regarding practice without impact on doctrine. The denominations showed this with their sacraments, which became the "means of grace," and their creeds, which became sources of authority. Certainly the nondenominational churches, in their effort to eliminate any uncomfortable controversy, have altered not only the work of the church, but the doctrine which it is charged to support.

Another issue that the nondenominational churches bring to the forefront is the result of a shallow theology. In her book entitled *Almost Christian,* Kenda Creasy Dean draws from the *National Study of Youth in Religion* (a research project conducted by the University of Notre Dame), in which over 3000 adolescents were interviewed, and found that many teenagers today "enact and espouse a religious outlook that is distinct from traditional teachings of most world religions," which she calls "moralistic therapeutic deism." Dean defines this as a religious view that "helps people be nice, feel good, and leaves God in the background" (21).[3] She noted that the majority of teenagers they spoke to were "incredibly inarticulate about their faith, their religious beliefs and practices, and its meaning

3 Dean, Kenda Creasy. *Almost Christian: What the Faith of Our Teenagers is Telling the American Church*, Oxford University Press, 2010.

or place in their lives" (18). Many of these teens could not describe their religious beliefs at all, either claiming not to have any or describing views deemed heretical by their particular denomination. She goes on to say, "Perhaps young people lack robust Christian identities because churches offer such a stripped-down version of Christianity that it no longer poses a viable alternative to imposter spiritualities like Moralistic Therapeutic Deism" (36). In light of this trend it should come as no surprise that the nondenominational churches are struggling to keep members age 30-49, showing a 7% decrease from 2007-2014, as did the Baptist church.

Whether we are speaking of the Baptist church and the youth group movement, the Methodist church and the focus on Social Justice, the hyper-emotionalism of the Pentecostal churches, or the come-as-you-are-stay-as-you-came adaptability of the nondenominational churches, the failure to present the Gospel as a mold by which we must shape our lives leaves people unprepared to face the harsh realities of life in a sin corrupted world. The anemic faith that such teaching produces is often the first victim.

What should we take away from this trend? Should churches of Christ continue to use the term "nondenominational" to describe local churches? Some may call for a change in our language so that people do not connect our congregations to these secular institutions. Which term should we abandon, "nondenominational" or "church"? This may

> A denominational church is any church that demonstrates a willingness to change the pattern of Scripture in either doctrine or practice.

sound facetious, but what would such a change actually accomplish? We might adopt terms such as "anti-denominational" or "pre-denominational" but the issue is not language but practice. Rather than giving up good terminology, we may be better served to use the opportunity to speak about why we differ from the other nondenominational churches in town.

Secondly, we must recognize that the denominational mindset is not limited to those associated with a traditional denomination. A denominational church is any church that demonstrates a willingness to change the pattern of Scripture in either doctrine or practice, which is why we have referred to the "Non-denominational Denomination." This is the core issue that every church must guard against. In order to accomplish this, it is essential that each successive generation is able to identify areas of liberty and areas of doctrinal importance.

Furthermore any change in tradition that is made must be carefully considered. Local churches need to ascertain what led to a particular practice and, if it is determined to be a mere tradition, there needs to be an understanding of what principle of Scripture may have been upheld, defended, or clarified through its practice. Underlying all of these things there must be an emphasis placed on spiritual education within local churches. There must be a concerted effort within local churches to encourage individuals to have a deeper understanding of God's word, to make the connection between theology and godly living, to have a greater understanding of hermeneutics and to grasp the "why" behind the "what" that we might retain that pattern of sound words. To pretend that this trend of cultural conformity and the rapid change it requires is a problem existing only outside of churches of Christ is to ignore our own history and the tremendous strides the more liberal institutional churches have taken away from the Divine pattern. It must be acknowledged that we live in a culture that denies any objective standards of right and wrong and the nondenominational denomination is certainly proving that such thinking can and will have incredible impact on churches. Local churches of Christ must take a proactive stand if they are to have any hope of standing fast.

SHAWN CHANCELLOR

Study Questions

1. What factors led to the rise of the Non-denominational Denomination? _____

2. Why do these churches place a priority on an emotional worship experience? _____

3. Why do these churches avoid "traditional doctrines" such as the need for baptism, the significance of the Lord's Supper, or the role of women in public worship? _____

4. What steps have these churches taken to allow for rapid changes in doctrine and practice? _____

5. In 1 Timothy 4, what did Paul command Timothy to do in regards to the false doctrines and practices that he would encounter? _____

6. According to 1 Timothy 3:15 what role does the church serve? Can a church fulfill this role without dealing with topics that might offend some people? _____

7. How does doctrine affect practice? Can one change the work of the church without changing the doctrine revealed in Scripture? _____

8. What effect does the absence of substantive preaching and teaching have on the faith of individuals in a local church? _____

9. What does "denominational" mean? Does this term suggest more than an affiliation with traditional denominations? _____

10. What steps can a local church take to resist the pressure our culture places upon it to make changes regarding faith and practice? _____

The "Church of Christ" Denomination

By Andrew Dow

There has always been a substantial portion of humanity that has defied God and insisted on doing things their own way. Perhaps no clearer picture of this exists than the one we find in Exodus 32-34. The newly freed Israelites had just agreed to enter a covenant with the Lord, twice stating, "All the words which the Lord has spoken we will do!" (Exod. 24:3, 7, NASB). At the Lord's command, Moses hiked up the mountain and received the instructions for the Tabernacle – the place where God would dwell among His people and, consequently, where His people would come to worship Him. While God was providing the instructions for this magnificent structure the people became antsy, threw together an idol, and worshipped that idol. The scene at the foot of the mountain was profoundly pathetic, and yet it is the picture of all men and women when they agree to worship and serve God but turn around only to disregard His direction.

> We live among people who openly proclaim, "All the words which the Lord has spoken we will do!" and yet they ignore His commands regarding salvation and they dismantle the design of His church.

This scenario is repeating itself among many of today's "Christians." We live among people who openly proclaim, "All the words which the Lord has spoken we will do!" and yet they ignore His commands regarding salvation, they reject His expectations in regards to personal conduct, and they dismantle the design of His church. God has handed down a pattern, which if followed, will grant us fellowship with Him. The so-called "Christians" around us have rejected this pattern and have instead substituted their own form of worship.

The above paragraph describes the denominational world around us, but this type of total disregard for the instructions of God is becoming increasingly more common among those who once broadcasted the "just Christians" mentality. David Edwin Harrell wrote a twenty-eight page booklet in 1962 in which he explained that, at that time, "a large segment of the church of Christ [was] well on the path toward denominational status" (*Emergence of the "Church of Christ" Denomination*, 23). A former Pepperdine University and Abilene Christian University professor, Richard T. Hughes, described the early

Cooperative program involving Baptist, Presbyterian, and Methodist churches with a "Church of Christ" in Amarillo, Texas.

twentieth century as the time in which he believes the "Church of Christ" Denomination came to fruition (*Reviving the Ancient Faith*, 137).

Some "Churches of Christ" now proudly proclaim themselves to be denominational. For example, a "Church of Christ" that is uniting with Baptist, Methodist, and Presbyterian churches wrote on their website, "We believe this partnership between denominations is a powerful witness to our city…" (*http://www.amarillocentral.org/#!4-amarillo/c1t8t*). Other "Churches of Christ" claim to be non- (or un-) denominational, but in reality cannot be differentiated from the denominations around them. This is the case when congregations support various para-church organizations (papers, schools, etc.), utilize women in public leadership roles, or offer fellowship to anyone who claims to be "a Christian." Both of these unfortunate situations make it difficult to convince the world that true "churches of Christ" (Rom. 16:16) are in no way a part of a denomination. It is for this reason that we would do well to consider a few things regarding what some have referred to as the "Church of Christ" denomination.

This Shouldn't Surprise Us!

It may be that we look around at the current conditions of local "churches of Christ" and are shocked to find denominational tendencies sneaking into these groups. Perhaps we see things changing in our own congregations that clearly indicate a shift toward denominational attitudes in the church. Do not allow these things to catch you by surprise!

God's Word teaches us that apostasy will take place. Apostasy was a recurring theme in Paul's letters to Timothy. "Remain on at Ephesus," he told the young preacher, "so that you may instruct certain men not to teach strange doctrines.... For some men, straying from these things, have turned aside..." (1 Tim. 1:3-7). Shortly thereafter Paul wrote, "In later times some will fall away from the faith" (1 Tim. 4:1-5). In another epistle Paul wrote words that eerily reflect our own society, "Difficult times will come. For men will be lovers of self, lovers of money, boastful... lovers of pleasure rather than lovers of God, holding to a form of godliness, although they have denied its power..." (2 Tim. 3:1-9).

Lest you think these warnings of apostasy are confined to one portion of Scripture, consider Paul's words to the shepherds over the flock in Ephesus – "I know that after my departure savage wolves will come in among you, not sparing the flock; and from among your own selves men will arise, speaking perverse things, to draw away the disciples after them" (Acts 20:29-30). Jude spoke with the same conviction and concern when he

said, "Certain persons have crept in unnoticed... ungodly persons who turn the grace of our God into licentiousness and deny our only Master and Lord, Jesus Christ" (Jude 4).

There are certainly other passages we could point to that contain these same types of warnings (e.g. Gal. 1:6-10; 2 Pet. 2:1-3; Titus 1:10-16; etc.), and we could spend much time discussing the correct historical application of each of these warnings. But what is there for us to learn from all of these warnings? As long as God has given laws for man to live by, man has found ways to disobey those laws. In the same way, we will encounter those today who have deserted God's pattern for the church in favor of man-made patterns. Don't be surprised that these things are happening; they have always happened and will continue to happen. Instead, know God's Word so that you can identify error and react appropriately.

Why Is This Happening and What Can We Do?

With the remainder of my allotted space, I'd like to consider these two questions: *"Why are once sound churches becoming more like denominations?"* and *"What can we do about this change?"* Accurately answering the first question will help us effectively answer the second. Allow me to offer just two of my own observations on the matter.

1. Denominations Appear Successful. In fact, one might say that, from a worldly perspective, denominations are incredibly successful! Denominations seem to attract great numbers of people, and receive great sums of money. It's not hard to understand why – from a worldly perspective, what is more appealing? Reverently praising God or a rock-n-roll concert? Remaining holy as God is holy or being accepted despite your worldly lifestyle? You see, denominations employ flashy and fleshly tactics to get people in their doors, and it works! Is it ever the case that we desire to have the same kind of worldly success that denominations enjoy?

> Denominations employee flashy and fleshly tactics to get people in their doors, and it works!

Scripture reveals a sharp contrast between man's perspective and God's. You may recall that, having seen Jesse's firstborn son Eliab, Samuel thought, "Surely the LORD's anointed is before Him" (1 Sam. 16:6). The Lord responded, "Do not look at his appearance or at the height of his stature, because I have rejected him; for God sees not as man sees, for man looks at the outward appearance, but the LORD looks at the heart" (1 Sam. 16:7). While man looks at outward, physical, observable characteristics to determine success, God's measure of success is not so carnal. Just as God revealed through the prophet Isaiah, "'My thoughts are not your thoughts, nor are your ways My ways,' declares the LORD" (Isa. 55:8).

So, how are we to respond? We must recognize how truly unsuccessful denominations are spiritually. We may look at various denominations and say, *"Surely the LORD's church is before Him."* After all, they appear to love God and they attract sizable crowds. *"Do not look at their appearance or at the size of their bank accounts ... for man looks at the outward appearance, but the LORD looks at the heart."* Earthly success is not success in God's eyes; do not let denominational "success" fool you into departing from the standard of God's Word.

2. People Desire to Please People. This general truth can be observed in just about any area of life. We want people to like and accept us, so we attempt to do things that we think they will like. Can this attitude bleed into our churches as well? Consider the various denominations around us: Why do some

> Why are churches swapping pulpits and extending fellowship to anyone who walks in their door? Is it because God commanded these activities or because these things please people?

NOTES

churches have traditional and contemporary worship services? Why do some churches offer youth groups, financial seminars, movie or game nights, softball teams, etc.? Why are churches swapping pulpits and extending fellowship to anyone and everyone who walks in their door? Is it because God has commanded His church to be involved in these activities, or is it because these things please people?

Christians are followers, slaves, and servants of Christ. Christ alone is to be our Lord. Paul asked, "Am I now seeking the favor of men, or of God? Or am I striving to please men? If I were still trying to please men, I would not be a bond-servant of Christ" (Gal. 1:10). When our desire is to please men, we cease to be slaves of Christ. To the contrary, we must become increasingly interested in pleasing God in the local church. If our aim is not to conform to His will, what makes us any different than any other social club aiming to be liked and accepted by men? We must adopt the attitude of the early Christians who explained, "we must obey God rather than men" (Acts 5:29).

Conclusion

To speak of the "Church of Christ" denomination is to use an oxymoron. Simply put, a local church that considers itself a part of a denomination or conducts itself as a denomination cannot properly be described as a church that belongs to Christ. It should not surprise us to find those who, while claiming to follow Christ, ignore God's clear instructions. However, if we measure success as God measures success and if our entire focus is on pleasing God, we can make sure that the local churches of which we are a part do not simply claim to be of Christ, but are in reality churches that belong to Christ!

ANDREW DOW

Study Questions

1. Take a closer look at Exodus 32-34. What are some ways in which you see the story of the golden calf being repeated in various churches today? _____
   _____
   _____

2. Why is it important that our local church avoids denominational distinctions? _____
   _____
   _____

3. What are some biblical examples of men falling short of God's Law? Are we any different today? ___
   _____
   _____
   _____

4. How does God measure success in His church? _____
   _____
   _____
   _____

5. What does a bond-servant of Christ look like? _____
   _____
   _____
   _____

6. Aside from the two points raised in this article, why else are churches of Christ becoming more like the denominations around them? _____
   _____
   _____
   _____

7. Based on your answers above, what can we do as a local church to guard against such tendencies?
   _____
   _____
   _____
   _____
   _____

The "Mega-Church" Mentality—*What Can the Church Do for Me?*

By Curtis Carwile

Is there a more American word than "mega"? That word perfectly describes what Americans love. We love to "Super-size" it. We love megaplexes. We love Texas. So, it shouldn't be any surprise that we love "mega-churches."

A mega-church is often defined as a religious group with certain identifying marks. For one, a mega-church will have, on average, over 2000 attendees per assembly. Also, a mega-church will have a charismatic and authoritative senior minister who runs their group like the CEO of a company (such as Joel Osteen and Rick Warren). And, they are always engaged in various social and aid-type "ministries."

Joel Osteen's Lakeland Church in Houston, Texas is currently the largest mega-church in the nation with a reported weekly attendance of 43,000.

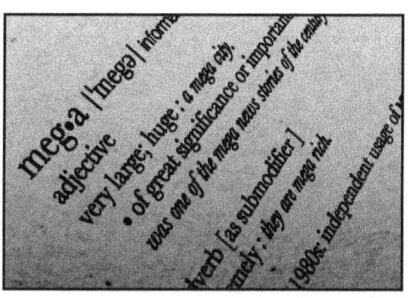

In the United States today, there are over 16,000 mega-churches. And, that number is growing because people see the (numerical) success of these groups and they imitate them to various degrees.

Now, while there is nothing wrong with the numerical size of a group (e.g., the church in Jerusalem had over 5000 members, see Acts 4:4), the mentality of these mega-churches, those groups wanting to be mega-churches, and those wanting to be a part of a mega-church is unnerving and unbiblical.

Very simply put, the mega-church mentality is this: BIGGER is better. This mentality has two consequential sides to it: the *producer* side and the *consumer* side.

The *PRODUCER* side of this mentality is what makes church leaders "do whatever it takes to get BIGGER." Unfortunately, and despite what they claim (cf. Matt. 7:21-23; Luke 6:46), this mentality has nothing to do with the actual glorification of God (which is what a church is supposed to be all about, see 1 Cor. 10:31). Rather, this mentality promotes the worship of size and numbers. To be blunt, this mentality is idolatrous. BIGGER is their goal. Their bellies are their gods (Phil. 3:17-18). This is why mega-churches do what they do. They want to attract as many people to them as possible and do whatever it takes to not run off anyone away from them (you see, it's all about them). This is why mega-churches soften their preaching to the level of pseudo-spiritual mush; they will never preach hard-to-hear truth (like Jesus did, see John 6:60ff) because they don't want to offend anyone (like Jesus did, see Luke 11:45) and "cause" them to leave. Also, this is why mega-churches make their "worship" assemblies "entertainment hours" with rocking bands, humorous skits and sketches, and dazzling multi-media presentations. By the way, isn't this the same type of thing Paul rebuked the Corinthians for doing in 1 Corinthians 14:26? And, this is why mega-churches build these huge, multi-campus facilities filled with goods instead of godliness (e.g., places with a bookstore and coffee shop in the lobby, a gym in the "fellowship hall," and a daycare school in their west wing), which is exactly the same type of thing Jesus railed against when He cleansed the Temple (see John 2:13-17). The producer side of this mentality is idolatry, plain and simple.

Likewise, the *CONSUMER* side of this mentality is also idolatrous. Because the member or attendee believes that "BIGGER is better," they look at the (mega)church as a (super)market, a place for their personal consumption. The main question of those with this mindset is "What can (or do) *I* get out of this?" You see, people flock to mega-churches to GET something out of it; it's all about THEM. And, while the attendee should receive the benefit of edification from a worship assembly and from being a part of a church (cf. Eph. 4:11-16), the mindset of "what can (or do) I GET out of this?" is wrong. It's self-centered instead of God-centered! It's sinful pride (see Rom. 1:30)! It goes against the humble, self-sacrificing mentality Christians are supposed to have (see Phil. 2:3-5). It goes against the God-glorifying and other-edifying mentality that the church is supposed to have (cf. 1 Cor. 10-14; Eph. 4:11-16). Again, it is nothing more than self-idolization at its core.

All in all, the mega-church mentality is wrong, sinful, and damnable. And, we, as individual Christians and churches, cannot have any fellowship with this mentality if we hope to have a fellowship with God here and in eternity (see 1 John 1:5-7).

> The mega-church mentality is alive and well even inside sound churches of Christ.

Unfortunately, I'm afraid that this mentality (one side of it or the other) has sneaked into even faithful churches of Jesus Christ (cf. 2 Pet. 2:1-3), more so than I'm sure we are comfortable admitting. We see it among us, don't we? We see it when preachers WON'T preach on a particular Bible topic (like homosexuality, divorce, drinking, institutionalism, church discipline, and even salvation in Jesus) because they don't want to offend someone. We see it when someone DOES preach the truth in love (Eph, 4:15) and someone leaves because he got his feelings hurt. We see it when someone leaves a sound church for social reasons. We see it when someone stops assembling because he or she is "just not getting anything out of it." And, we see it in so many other examples. So, yes, the mega-church mentality is alive and well, even inside sound churches of Christ.

With all of that said, what are we going to do about it? As a people of God, we cannot allow wickedness to persist and spread in the world around us (see Psa. 101:8); we must resolve ourselves against it. We must humbly and biblically examine ourselves to see if our mindset has been tainted in any way with it (cf. 2 Cor. 13:5). And, if we find any of this mentality in ourselves, then we must expeditiously rid ourselves of it; if we don't, then how can we ever hope to help others rid their thinking of it (see Matt. 7:1-5)? We must truly abhor this evil while loving with true love (1 Cor. 13) the lost souls who have been infected with this aberrant mentality (Rom. 12:9). As a result, we are going to take the Great Commission (Mark 16:15-16; Matt. 28:19-20) and the Bible example of what it means to be a disciple (see Acts 8:4; 20:27) to heart more than we ever have before and be busy tearing down the strongholds of Satan with the Sword of the Spirit (cf. 2 Cor. 10:3-6; Eph. 6:17; Heb. 4:12), winning lost souls back to God. And, we are going to do our best to glorify God and to edify our brethren in the Lord, sacrificing even our own lives to that end (cf. Rom. 12:1-2)! If we are going to defeat this evil, then we are going to do these things (as well as many other godly things) to the glory of God.

The mega-church mentality is a destructive and damnable heresy. Let us do whatever it takes to glorify God and help others do the same. And, may the Lord grant us strength, wisdom, and courage in our efforts.

CURTIS CARWILE

Study Questions

1. What is the work of the local church? _____

2. How do we determine what the work of the local church is? _____

3. What kind of musical worship are we to offer? Why? _____

4. What is the Social Gospel? Should it be taught in the local church? _____

5. Should we accept everyone as a member? Why not? _____

6. What are some legitimate concerns for members with larger groups? _____

7. What are some "ministries" a mega-church near you offers? _____

8. What is the "mega-church mentality"? What are the two sides of it? _____

9. What positive things can we learn from mega-churches? _____

10. What else can we do about the "mega-church mentality"? _____

"Let Your Women *Not* Be Silent in the Churches"
The Rise of Gender-Inclusion in the Mainstream
By Jason Garcia

I do not permit a woman to teach or to exercise authority over a man; rather, she is to remain quiet (1 Tim. 2:12, ESV).

The women are to keep silent in the churches; for they are not permitted to speak, but are to subject themselves, just as the Law also says (1 Cor. 14:34).

These verses are unapologetically straightforward. To be sure, there's more to say about these passages in their context (and we will), but even a cursory reading reveals clear and basic principles about how a woman must conduct herself toward men at all times and, specifically, in the church assembly. Sadly, what's become par for the course are creeds, policies, and headlines from churches that blatantly reject these passages. For example:

Canon Alison White

The Church of England has announced that the Rev. Canon Alison White will be consecrated as its second female bishop since the Church voted last year to allow women to become bishops (headline from *Christian Post*, Jan. 26, 2015).

Elizabeth Eaton

Clergywomen have been part of Methodism since John Wesley licensed Sarah Crosby to preach in 1761. Although women were ordained in the Methodist tradition as early as the late 1800s, it was the May 4, 1956 General Conference vote for full clergy rights that forever changed the face of ordained clergy (*umc.org*, official website of the United Methodist Church).

The Evangelical Lutheran Church in America elected Rev. Elizabeth Eaton as its first female presiding bishop in 2013 (story from *Huffington Post*, Sept. 26, 2014).

This is nothing new. All denominations have raced toward social acceptance from day one. In fact, that's precisely why many of them have been established – to fill a popular social niche. In this they strive to outdo one another, ever upping the ante and doubling down on their acceptance of whatever fad society and popular culture hold forth as the new norm. So, naturally they hastened to be swept up in the momentum created by ideologies, which cry "foul" over scripturally defined gender roles. Like so many false teachings, the gender-inclusive movement among denominations (that's been around for centuries) has spilled over into the church. There's even a website dedicated to cataloging so-called churches of Christ which identify themselves as "gender-inclusive." They couch themselves as the antithesis of those naughty churches that "practice discrimination" and "exclusion." Unashamedly, they allow women to serve as elders, deacons, evangelists, or to fill the pulpit in some leading role within an assembly. What really speaks to their delusion is the name of their website: *wherethespiritleads.org*. I guess when you're trying to snooker the naive and unstable, "where the spirit leads" sounds better than *"i-categorically-reject-the-biblical-pattern.*

Three Popular Female Denominational Preachers

Beth Moore is an "evangelist" and founder of Living Proof Ministries based in Houston. She is a regular speaker on the television program LIFE Today.

Holly Wagner is a "lead pastor" and co-founder of Oasis Church, a "non-denominational" church in Los Angeles.

Nadia Bolz-Weber is the coarse, foul-mounthed, founding "pastor" of House for All Sinners and Saints, an Evangelical Lutheran church in Denver.

org." But should we really be surprised? The truth is many congregations were already in the ditch on this issue long before women were paraded out as "preaching interns." When churches of Christ began to allow women to read Scripture or lead prayers in a mixed assembly, or serve the Lord's supper, or be part of a "praise team" (wherein a few men and women collectively lead singing), what did we think would be the next step? If we aren't careful we might soon find ourselves among brethren who look at the myriads of "gender-inclusive" churches and say, "Well, why not?"

Let's take another look at those fundamentally important passages that speak to this issue:

1 Corinthians 14:33-35 is *not* teaching that in the event a woman fails to remain absolutely silent and breathes so much as a whisper in the assembly, she sins. The word *sigaō* (σιγάω) means silent (cf. Acts 12:17; 15:12), but it is not totally unqualified in our context. If it is totally unqualified, then many of us are in trouble because our women speak in every assembly. How so? Does not the Holy Spirit describe singing psalms, hymns, and spiritual songs as "speaking to one another" (Eph. 5:18-20; cf. Col. 3:16)?

Furthermore, if a woman after hearing the Gospel in an assembly decides she wants to obey and comes forward to be baptized and is asked, "Do you believe with all of your heart that Jesus Christ is the Son of God?" What's she going to say? She had better say, "Yes" or something equivalent, or else things are going to come to a grinding halt. She can't just silently nod her head and expect that to be okay. Paul said, "if you confess with your MOUTH Jesus as Lord, and believe in your heart that God raised Him from the dead, you will be saved; for with the heart a person believes, resulting in righteousness, and with the MOUTH he confesses, resulting in salvation" (Rom. 10:9-10, emphasis mine).

So very quickly we begin to see that, if we interpret Paul's words in 1 Corinthians 14:34-35 to mean an unqualified kind of silence – that a woman literally can't breathe a word in the assembly – then that means she couldn't sing as commanded, she couldn't make the good confession (which Paul reveals might be in the presence of many witness, 1 Tim. 6:12), and she couldn't verbally correct her children when they misbehave. An unnecessary host of issues is created as we're spun off into all kinds of contradictions and inconsistencies and unscriptural teaching.

> Paul prohibits a certain kind of speaking—a woman in a mixed assembly who takes control of the assembly to address and speak to the congregation, just as the tongue-speaker and prophet would.

The fact is women speak in every assembly all of the time in their obedience to Ephesians 5:19 because the Bible's prohibition on women speaking in the assembly is not categorical. The immediate context makes this clear when the same word, *sigaō* (σιγάω) is used in v. 28 in regard to the tongue speaker. If there wasn't an interpreter, then he was to keep silent. We ask, "Keep absolutely silent in what way?" In so far as exercising that gift. He could still sing and he could still say "amen" (v. 16) at the end of a prayer, because the command to keep silent applied specifically to speaking in different languages when there was no one to translate. The prophet is given the same command when a different situation arose, but the point remains the same (vv. 29-30).

The subject under discussion in the context of 1 Corinthians 12-14 is the exercise of miraculous gifts before the whole assembly. Thus we should understand "speak" in this context as addressing, thereby leading and exercising authority over, the church assembled (1 Cor. 14:27-30). The male tongue-speaker, without an interpreter, and the prophet were both instructed to "keep silent," and were forbidden to address the assembly in the specified situation. Women are told not to speak *at all* in that specific authoritative, leading capacity in the assembly.

Was Paul's justification cultural? Obviously not, because the rationale given is it is "improper for a woman to speak in church" – a principle carried over from the Old Law (vv. 34-35). Again, Paul has in mind a certain kind of speaking—a woman in a mixed assembly who takes control of the assembly to address and speak to the congregation, just as the tongue-speaker and prophet would. Bear in mind, too, this can be done without a woman ever coming to the pulpit. For example, a woman can try to lead an assembly in song or prayer or teaching from the pew, or try to make comments during announcements about the sick or a meal schedule, etc. This too, would violate 1 Corinthians 14:33-35 as well as 1 Timothy 2:11-12 where it is abundantly clear that a woman cannot exercise authority over a man. However...

1 Timothy 2:11-12 does *not* say that a woman can never teach a man. Take for instance the example we have in Acts 18:26. Apollos began to speak boldly in the synagogue, but when Priscilla and Aquila heard him, they took him aside and explained to him the way of God more accurately. *They* took him aside. It's indisputable that both Aquila and Priscilla taught Apollos the way of God more accurately. Women *can* teach men in certain contexts. What 1 Timothy 2 prohibits is a certain manner of teaching from a woman, but not all

NOTES

Women's Restrictions in the New Testament and Their Context

1 Corinthians 14:34-35	1 Timothy 2:11-12	Acts 18:24-26
Context: Spiritual gifts and conduct in the assembly of the church.	**Context:** General conduct—not specifically the assembly of the church.	**Context:** A private meeting outside of an assembly of the church.
Command: "Keep silent"	**Command:** Learn in "quietness" (ASV) or "quietly" (NASB).	**Example:** "They took him aside" and (in the Greek) "they explained to him the way of God more accurately."
Prohibition: A woman is not permitted to speak when the congregation is assembled as a church.	**Prohibition:** In general conduct a woman may not teach or exercise authority over a man.	**Necessary Inference:** In a setting outside of the assembly of the church (such as a Bible class) a woman may discuss spiritual things with those other than her husband, while maintaining a submissive and quiet disposition.

teaching. The issue in 1 Timothy 2:11-12 is not the formality or informality of a setting as some have argued (i.e. a woman can never teach in a formal class setting). That's not the issue. Titus 2:3-4 teaches that women should be teachers of good things and teach other women. Various settings can be used to expediently fulfill this (even in an appropriate, formal Bible class setting). 1 Timothy 2:11-12 prohibits the exercising of authority over a man. Again, Paul is not saying that a woman may never teach a man. If a lady were to come up to the preacher after an assembly and want to discuss the sermon, and maybe she has some insight or some other passages to suggest, should he say, "No! Wait! Stop! Don't tell me that, because then you would be teaching me"? Of course not.

We must keep these scriptural limitations within their context, avoiding the equally fatal errors of wresting them to oppress women or ignoring them altogether. If you read the justifications from those who advocate women preaching, you'll quickly discover that, according to them, God hates women and is just trying to hold them back.

God is not keeping any of us from some great work, and He certainly has not short changed women. What He has done is given men *and* women specific work to do in the Kingdom (1 Cor. 12:14-20). Remember, there are limitations on men and women, but we all have much God-glorifying work to do within the sphere designated for us by God. So let's find our place and role, and use our gifts in accordance with the Scripture.

JASON GARCIA

Study Questions

1. How do the prohibitions for the prophet and tongue speaker help us better understand the regulation given to women in the church assembly? _____
   _____
   _____
   _____
   _____

2. The charge from "gender-inclusive" churches is that congregations practice discrimination and exclusion when they impose gender restrictions and forbid women to preach, lead prayers or songs, or make announcements in a mixed assembly. How would you answer this charge? Are women really being mistreated by remaining silent or filling biblically designated roles? _____
   _____
   _____
   _____
   _____

3. Is Paul's instruction for women to "remain silent in the churches" culturally biased and motivated? What in the context of 1 Cor. 14 and 1 Tim. 2 demonstrate the rationale for this instruction? _____
   _____
   _____
   _____
   _____

4. If a woman is to remain silent in the church, does this mean she may never teach a man? Why or why not? Can you give specific, scriptural examples? If there are circumstances in which a woman may teach a man, what must she remember from 1 Tim. 2? Are there any other passages that speak to the capacity in which a woman must teach? _____
   _____
   _____
   _____
   _____

5. A common passage used to support the gender-inclusive movement is Gal. 3:28. What is the context of this verse and the main thrust of Paul's teaching? _____
   _____
   _____
   _____
   _____

6. In an attempt to shore up their argument, the gender-inclusive movement often points to the women in their churches who no longer feel inadequate or useless. Their assumption is these feelings are directly related to the instructions in 1 Cor. 14 and 1 Tim. 2. What can we do (men and women) to avoid the pitfalls of feeling useless or uninvolved? _____
   _____
   _____
   _____
   _____

The Moral Fog of Modern Religion

By Bruce Reeves

When I was ten years old my parents took me on a tour of a cave in Branson, Missouri and it made quite the impression on me. As we were walking deeper and deeper into the recesses of the cave, our guide turned off the lights to show us how dark it was without any lighting. I literally could not see my hand in front of my face. Trying to find our way out without the lights on would have been impossible. In many ways the modern religious community is in a similar position. The present religious world has turned the lights off and is now stumbling around and making arbitrary statements about morality, yet having chosen a course that is doomed for blind conformity to an immoral and godless culture. We can read of Israel adopting such spiritual blindness as well, "In those days there was no king in Israel; everyone did what

was right in his own eyes" (Judg. 21:25, NASB). Likewise, Isaiah wrote, "Woe to those who call evil good, and good evil; who substitute darkness for light and light for darkness; who substitute bitter for sweet and sweet for bitter! Woe to those who are wise in their own eyes and clever in their own sight" (Isa. 5:20-21).

The Emerging Morality of Modern Religion

A secular writer doing an article on the Emerging Church movement summed up the character of the movement this way: "What makes a postmodern ministry so easy to embrace is that it doesn't demonize youth culture… like traditional fundamentalists. Postmodern congregants aren't challenged to reject the outside world."[1] The relativism and subjectivity of many professing Christians today on fundamental moral and Biblical issues may be perplexing to some, but it is a predictable outgrowth of those who are obsessed with cultural affirmation at all costs (cf. 1 Cor. 1:18-31).

Dr. Gene Veith, former Associate Professor of English at Concordia University-Wisconsin, argues that this all results in "postmodernism assuming that there is no objective truth, that moral values are relative, and that reality is socially constructed" by various "communities."[2] Veith then explains, "Whereas modernism sought to rid the world of religion, postmodernism spawns new ones. Unconstrained by objectivity, tradition, reason, or morality, these new faiths differ radically from Christianity. They have drawn on strains of the most ancient and primitive paganism." How did religious groups, which in times past were much more conservative on moral questions, end up where they are today?

The Suppression of Truth Is the Cause of Moral Confusion

This moral fog should not be a surprise to Christians. The suppression of the truth of God and the rejection of the authority of biblical revelation inescapably lead to moral chaos even among those who claim to be following the Lord. Paul wrote that there would be those who

> The suppression of the truth of God and the rejection of the authority of biblical revelation inescapably leads to moral chaos even among those who claim to be following the Lord.

---

1 Lori Leibovich, "Generation: A Look Inside Fundamentalism's Answer to MTV: ThePostmodern Church," 77.
2 Gene Veith, Jr., *Postmodern Times: A Christian Guide to Contemporary Thought and Culture* [Wheaton: Crossway, 1994], 193, cf. 198, 199.

were "lovers of pleasure rather than lovers of God, holding to a form of godliness, although they have denied its power" (2 Tim. 3:5). Jesus identified the tendency of the religious leaders of His day to replace the word of God with their own human traditions (Matt. 15:7-9). When truth is suppressed and man fails to acknowledge God, human pride brings forth the harvest of moral degeneration (Rom. 1:18-32). Paul's point in the first chapter of Romans is that sin damages man's entire direction and orientation, which comes from a proper recognition of the Lord.

The irony here is that while men claim to be wise, their lives actually demonstrate the contrary, i.e. moral confusion. Paul writes, "For even though they knew God, they did not honor Him as God or give thanks, but they became futile in their speculations, and their foolish heart was darkened. Professing to be wise they became fools" (Rom. 1:21, 22). When the glory, power, and morality of God are diminished, the status of humanity as God's creation is also diminished. The true motivation of idolatry is seen in much of the religious world today as one observes the suppression of the truth, the falsification of the reality of God, and the attitude which discounts God as a factor in the shaping of our lives. As a result of the removal of God from the discussion regarding sexual ethics and morality in general, humanity sinks further and further into depravity (Rom. 1:24-28).

Flawed Hermeneutic Has Practical Effects

Our commitment to the integrity, inspiration, and authority of the Bible, as well as our willingness to surrender to the instruction of the Lord has a deep influence on the stand we will take on moral questions. The hermeneutical approach that has been applied to a variety of doctrinal issues ranging from the organization and mission of the local church to the worship of God's people is also being applied to stances on sexuality. It is important that we identify not only the reality of the moral confusion of the religious world, but why this condition exists. It emanates from our understanding of "truth."

Once the testimony of Scripture is dismissed for subjective feelings as the criteria of establishing truth there is no logical stopping point. Recently the Fourth Avenue church of Christ in Franklin, TN began a preaching internship for a young woman, Lauren King. Consider some of the reasons she said she knew it was the will of God for her to preach publicly among God's people: "The Lord made it very clear to me through prayer and discernment that I

The Fourth Avenue church first began in 1833 in connection with the work of men such as Alexander Campbell and Tolbert Fanning with members committed to follow the "apostles' teaching" and the "ancient order."

should put an emphasis on preaching ... the way I perceive the Lord's will is when I have peace ... when I have peace the Lord is telling me 'Yes.'"[3]

Likewise, in 2006, the Richland Hills church of Christ in Fort Worth, Texas made "history" by incorporating the use of instrumental music in their worship. In a sermon delivered on December 10, 2006, Rick Atchley made the following statement regarding his reasoning: "Right there at that spot about 1994 the Holy Spirit said to me in the middle of my sermon, 'and that is what you and all the preachers like you were doing, who have not for years believed that the worship of God with instruments is wrong. But you continue by your silence to let people think its wrong....'"[4]

Rick Atchley

In a similar way the replacement of the objective standard of Scripture with a man-centered approach to the determination of God's will was seen several years ago regarding same-sex relationships. Gene Robinson defended the acceptance of those practicing homosexuality by appealing to direct and on-going revelation of the Holy Spirit, "Is there any doubt in your minds that the Holy Spirit is alive and well and calling God's Church to open itself to all those whom Jesus loves? We don't worship a God who is all locked up in Scripture 2000 years ago" (Robinson, 2006). According to Cathy Lynn Grossman of *USA Today* in an article entitled, "Gay Episcopal Bishop says, 'Holy Spirit Led Us,'" Robinson once again attributed his position regarding homosexuality (in spite of scriptural condemnation of such conduct) to his belief in the progressive leading of the Holy Spirit.

Gene Robinson

She went on to report the following in the same article, "The openly gay Episcopal bishop whose ordination threatens to fracture the worldwide Anglican Communion said Wednesday he 'genuinely and deeply regrets' the pain this caused some believers, but he sees no need to repent because 'the Holy Spirit led us.'" It is critical for us to recognize that the moral fog in modern religion today did not begin with the issues before us, but in a faulty approach to the Scriptures. This grows out of an effort to personalize God into our god, rather than allowing Him to reign as Sovereign.

Selective Hearing and Superficial Preaching

The moral fog in the religious community today has been produced by an arbitrary selection of hearing and preaching on a variety of moral questions. For instance, while the Bible is very clear regarding the sin of homosexuality, the Scripture is also

> The moral fog in the religious community today has been produced by an arbitrary selection of hearing and preaching on a variety of moral questions.

---

[3] Terry Francis http://eastshelby.com/resources/blog/2014/12/18/a-female-intern

[4] Rick Atchley (December 10, 2006). *Sermons on Podcasts, The Both/And Church.* Retrieved September 1, 2015, from Richland Hills Church of Christ: www.rhchurch.org

pointed regarding fornication of all kinds (1 Cor. 7:2). Any sexual relationship outside of marriage is sinful and should be addressed with vigilance. Likewise the problem of divorce is plaguing our families and communities (Matt. 5:32; 19:9). It is important that the biblical presentation is expressed in a balanced and thorough manner. Opposition to unbiblical notions must be proclaimed in a well-informed and productive way. The lack of contextual and substantive teaching does nothing to equip young Christians to engage the lost on controversial topics that are fundamental to the faith of Christ. The market-driven approach by many in the religious world has brought about the downward spiral of the religious world at large. Al Mohler commented on these trends in the Southern Baptist Denomination. He wrote:

> Churches in many ways have actually, I think, added to the problem. They promote the idea of the church as a full-service entertainment and activity center, where you take children away from their parents and just put them in a different peer culture. Now it's a church peer culture. What happens when they grow out of that? Kids are spending a very small amount of time in church activities, and many of those activities have very little theological, biblical or spiritual content. As a result, we have a generation of young people who believe that there is a God, but they don't have any particular god in mind. The pulpit has to take responsibility. In far too many churches there is just no expository preaching (teaching that expounds on a particular text of Scripture). There isn't the robust biblical preaching that sets forth the Word of God and then explains how the people of God are going to have to think differently and live differently in order to be faithful to that Word of God.[5]

What should we learn? One cannot start out with an unhealthy approach to the Bible and end up in a consistently scriptural place. Also, we cannot cherry-pick those issues we desire to address and ignore others of vital moral significance. The only solution is to give our all to proclaim the gospel of Christ to a lost world. The answer is not a palatable gospel that fits with the carnal desires of the unredeemed, but a transformative gospel, which is counter-cultural in our sanctification in Christ.

BRUCE REEVES

---

5 Mike Matthews and Dr. R. Albert Mohler, Jr., "Church Needs Change," (September 27, 2009), https://answersingenesis.org/christianity/church/does-church-need-change/.

Study Questions

1. What are some of the current issues today that demonstrate the fact that many are rejecting God's standards of living? _____
   _____
   _____
   _____

2. What are some fundamental reasons why the modern day religious community has become so confused on moral issues concerning sexuality? _____
   _____
   _____
   _____

3. How did Gene Robinson defend the acceptance of homosexuality? Did he appeal to Scripture? ____
   _____
   _____
   _____

4. Is there a relationship between how the religious world approaches doctrinal issues regarding the organization of the church and worship of God's people and present day moral questions? _____
   _____
   _____
   _____

5. What does Paul mean when he says some "suppress the truth"? _____
   _____
   _____
   _____

6. How did religious groups, which in times past were much more conservative on moral questions, end up where they are today? _____
   _____
   _____
   _____

7. What do you think God's people should learn from the moral fog of our religious friends? _____
   _____
   _____
   _____
   _____
   _____

"Nones" and "Dones"—The Rise of Non-Religious Religion

By Brian Haines

The Pew Research Center released a report in 2012 titled "'Nones' on the Rise" which noted the increase of those Americans who self-identify as having no religious affiliation (called "*nones*" by the study). A similar demographic (noted by sociologist Josh Packard in his book *Church Refugees*) exists as perhaps a subset of this first group that is identified as "*dones*," called such because of their decision to end a pre-existing religious affiliation. These two groups ("*nones*" and "*dones*") represent a growing trend in American culture of those who are non-participants in churches or worship services, but still have some identity of religion. They are neither atheists nor agnostics, but see themselves as unstructured believers.

They would likely identify themselves as "spiritual" but not "religious." Chances are, as this group grows, you have met them, and potentially seen brethren drift into this classification.

What has led to this growing trend? The Pew Research study revealed the "*nones*" and "*dones*" are composed fundamentally of persons of the most recent generation. It also revealed that the movement's numbers reflect a corresponding loss in membership in mainstream Protestant denominations. This might clue us in to the core ideology that programmed members of this movement in its formative years; presumably the fundamental unifying Protestant dogma of "*saved by faith alone*" would be the basis of faith from which this new demographic emerged. This movement then was entirely predictable. It is a natural conclusion that if faith is personal and emotional, then the person who is mindful towards God is spiritually successful regardless of his or her religious engagement with other believers. Why engage with the more difficult aspects of faith (i.e., works, particularly those of spiritual communing) if the entirety of the value of faith is found without works? If a person is told he will be paid regardless of his labors, it is almost certain that his labors will cease. Thus, the death of formal worship (even unauthorized) among many is a clear offspring of the easy-believism of recent generations. Wisdom *is* proven by its children; the worldly wisdom children (Jas. 3:15) of "*faith only*" are "*none*" and "*done.*"

Can a person be spiritual but not religious? Among worldly theologians and denominations the term "religion" has fallen out of favor. Even among our more liberal brethren that word has been minimalized. One apostate brother writes, "One aspect of religion is that it holds people in bondage. God has no religion. Christ did not die for a religion. The apostles did not establish a religion."[1] Yet Scripture uses the word "religion" (in Greek, *thrēskeia*, ceremonial observance) to describe the core actions of a Christian (Jas. 1:26-27). What many mean by their mindset (that they are spiritual but not religious) is that their faith is based entirely in emotion, which is nothing new (Prov. 14:12; Jer. 17:9; Prov. 28:26).

Additionally, their religion (for indeed, according to Colossians 2:23, their ideology is a religion) is one which rejects the communal nature of faith and instead makes faith a purely private and individual thing. Scriptures tell us that spirituality is not an

---

1 Dusty Owens, *Why I Left the Church of Christ*, the examiner.org, Volume 8, No. 6.

emotional personal condition, but a condition in which one has conformed himself to a greater truth of the Divine revelation (1 Cor. 2:14 – 3:1). Ironically, while the "*nones*" and "*dones*" may see themselves as spiritual but not religious, in fact Scripture says they are religious but not spiritual.

Engaging those who are on this road requires a degree of discernment, as there may be more than one underlying reason for being "*none*" and "*done.*" Many Christians were once lost among the denominations, and they too were discouraged by the "politics" or inexplicable conduct of these man-made institutions. We might conclude that some have ventured into this mindset lacking a knowledge of what primitive Christianity is all about. On the other hand, there are those who simply lack the intellectual work ethic to make application of the demands of faith. In a society that has become more focused on only engaging in activities that bring immediate and personal satisfaction, the delayed gratification mindset required of true spirituality is now rejected. To the first group we can offer genuine substantive belief, as Philip offered the Ethiopian Eunuch in Acts 8. On the other hand, with others we are dealing with the rich young ruler of Matthew 19 who wanted a faith that was tailored to him rather than a means of reconciliation to which he would need to submit. Jude makes the point in Jude 22-23 that we need to make a discernment in our approach to the lost; Philip chased the Ethiopian Eunuch, but Jesus let the rich young ruler depart.

It does not take a great deal of explanation to demonstrate that morality requires an absolute standard to have value. Jesus made numerous statements to the singular nature of truth (John 14:6), obedience (John 3:5), and salvation itself (Matt. 7:21-23). The "*nones*" and "*dones*" have come to believe that justification is an internal process – thus, righteousness is actually self-righteous, and their religion is one which they have created themselves. As we noted earlier, Paul makes this thinking his target in Colossians 2:23 when he says that "these are matters which have, to be sure, the appearance of wisdom in self-made religion." Those who reject Scriptural formality in faith lack any objective standard. We are witnesses in Scripture of the result of self-made religion when we consider the people of Israel in Judges, who, we are told, failed because everyone did what was right in their own eyes (Judg. 17:6; 21:25). Ignorance of the nature of truth and the nature of God is the core error (Hos. 4:6).

But perhaps most important to this discussion is the absolute that is stated by Paul in Romans 14:7 – "For none of us lives to himself, and no one dies to himself." True Christianity is a lifestyle that is at its core communal; how can one read Paul's admonition that we "bear one another's burdens, and thereby fulfill the law of Christ" (Gal. 6:2) and see ourselves as singular in our faith? How can we miss that Christianity is *fundamentally* a cooperative effort when there are 56 passages in the New Testament that demand our devoted attention to "one-another"? These core passages such as "love one another," "give preference to one another," "accept one another," "serve one another," or "be subject to one another" have the obvious implication of a close relationship in the church environment. Contextually, these commandments are to the members of the local church (as clarified in Eph. 4:25 with the expression "we are members of one another"). Christianity is a team-sport, and the mindset of the "*none*" and "*done*" is that of people who claim to play but won't join the team. When Jesus described the Day of Judgment in Matthew 25:31-46, He made it clear that a particularly important (indeed, in that passage, the only measurement) question for a believer is in regards to our supportive and familial engagement with other believers.

> When we come down to it, our "none" and "done" friends are simply renaming the ancient error that has afflicted believers from the first century onward: forsaking the assembly (Heb. 10:26).

When we come down to it, our "none" and "done" friends are simply renaming the ancient error that has afflicted believers from the first century onward: forsaking the assembly (Heb. 10:26). It may be that their hesitation to engage is based on legitimate issues. Denominational churches have become a mockery of worship and appear to be fundamentally focused on separating their members from their money. Sadly, we have witnessed digression in the Lord's church in these same areas in the last century. It may be that our "none" and "done" friends are worldly minded and selfish. One personal study I recently had concluded with a gentleman refusing to obey the Gospel because he did not want to be bound to other believers in a relationship of expectations. We must make it clear to ourselves (to prevent a falling away) and others that Jesus *died* to purchase the church (Acts 20:28); if the church relationship is unimportant, then Jesus died in vain (Gal. 2:21). Our relationship with God is repeatedly defined as being fundamentally tied to our relationship with other Christians – "beloved, let us love one another, for love is from God; and everyone who loves is born of God and knows God. The one who does not love does not know God, for God is love" (1 John 4:7-8). They might claim that they do love others, but what they mean is that they do not hate others; yet love is defined in the Bible in terms of our active engagement with others (1 Cor. 13:4-7), often specifically within terms of the church family, as we see in the context of the "one-another" passages of the New Testament.

Our review of the "*none*" and "*done*" trend has revealed several important points. First, we saw that this movement is born of "once saved, always saved" theology. As Jesus told us, we can know if something is from God by its fruit. We also saw that many who have come to see themselves as either having no religious affiliation or as being done with formal religion do so either because of their frustration over the worldliness of denominations (frustration with which we can sympathize) or it is born of pure self-righteousness. In contrast, we searched the divine word and found that our faith is not a matter of personal interpretation, but that there are absolute standards to which we must conform ourselves. We also have examined the New Testament revelation of the absolute importance of maintaining a communal relationship with brethren and with God through the church. We have understood that the maintenance of such a relationship is a key part of our final judgment.

BRIAN HAINES

Study Questions

1. Is it appropriate for Christians to identify themselves as religious? _____

2. What personal benefits do people find in an ideology of non-identification of faith? _____

3. What makes emotions so dangerous to be the basis our personal faith? _____

4. How would we make the case that morality is absolute and not relative or subjective? _____

5. What are some of the "absolute" statements that Jesus and His disciples have made about Christianity? _____

6. In what manner is Christianity a group relationship with God? In what way is Christianity a personal relationship with God? Are these ideas mutually exclusive? What errors arise when one relationship (personal or group) is elevated over another? _____

7. How might the denominational financial pattern drive many to the "none" and "done" mindset? What lesson is there for us in this (Matt. 7:16-17)? _____

8. What teachings about communion in 1 Corinthians 11:17-34 (and elsewhere) reveal that observing this memorial requires a constant relationship with other believers? _____

From *Sola Scriptura* to *Nulla Scriptura*

By Melvin Curry

The Protestant Reformation

Despite many apostasies, horrific wars, and social upheavals, the church in both the East and West continued the careful transmission of the Scriptures from generation to generation. Even following the Protestant Reformation, the numerous independent churches attempted to keep one another in check through an appeal to the authority of the written word. The leaders of the Reformation held in common two distinctive doctrines: (1) the way to God is through faith in Jesus Christ, not through "any human mediator," such as pope or priest; and (2) the Bible is the "final authority" for doctrine.[1] These fundamental principles came to be called in Latin *sola fide* ("faith only") and *sola scriptura* ("Scripture only").

The reformers firmly believed what the Bible affirms about itself: "All Scripture is inspired of God, and is profitable for doctrine, for reproof, for correction, for instruction in righteousness" (2 Tim. 3:16). These spiritually-minded men accepted God's word as "truth" (John 17:17) and affirmed the Scriptures to be divine "oracles" (1 Pet. 4:11). They recognized the Bible to be God's "revelation," which He had made known to mankind through His chosen messengers (Eph. 3:3; cf. 1 Thess. 2:13; 1 Cor. 2:12-13). It was not the product of man's will but of God's Spirit, who "moved" men to write its words (2 Pet. 1:20-21). Therefore, the Scriptures must not to be amplified or diminished (Deut. 4:2; cf. 5:32; Rev. 22:19).[2] The reformers tried to live by the commandment, "Man shall not live by bread alone, but by every word that proceeds from the mouth of God" (Matt. 4:4; cf. Deut. 8:3).

Martin Luther: "Unless I am convinced by the testimony of the Scriptures or by clear reason (for I do not trust either in the pope or in councils alone, since it is well known that they have often erred and contradicted themselves), I am bound by the Scriptures I have quoted and my conscience is captive to the Word of God." Before the Diet of Worms, April 18, 1521.

Nevertheless, reformation meant different things to each of the reformers. On the one hand, Martin Luther retained many things that were not expressly forbidden in the Scriptures, but he held that the Bible is the final authority instead of the church. One of his greatest achievements was to translate the Bible into the language of ordinary German people. On the other hand, John Calvin sought to exclude what could not be proved by the teaching of the New Testament. Nevertheless, he filtered the Scriptures through the lens of Augustinian theology (total depravity, unconditional election, limited atonement, irresistible grace, and perseverance of the saints). John Wesley and the Methodists firmly believed in the inspiration of the Scriptures and particularly focused on what they considered the Holy Spirit's second work of grace, namely, the entire sanctification of believers. The Anabaptist churches likewise held a deep respect for the Bible. They, more nearly than the other groups within Protestantism, restored the church to the New Testament pattern. Many of them, however, displayed mystical tendencies and fanatical premillennial beliefs.[3]

> The reformers tried to live by the commandment, "Man shall not live by bread alone, but by every word that proceeds from the mouth of God" (Matt. 4:4; cf. Deut. 8:3).

---

[1] Cairns. *Modern Church History* (Zondervan, 1981), 2:284.

[2] Martin Luther, however, wrestled with the authority of Hebrews, James, Jude, and Revelation because they appeared to go against his doctrine of *sola fide* (faith only).

[3] Albert H. Newman provides a good summary of the major

The fertile soil of the Renaissance had produced a "rebirth" of culture that exerted both positive and negative influences on the Protestant Reformation. It awakened Europe to the study of Greek and Hebrew and produced the printing press, yet it unleashed many excesses of human reason and feeling. It eventually gave way to the Enlightenment of the seventeenth and eighteenth centuries, with its liberalizing effect on religious thought. More and more, man became the measure of all things.

Modernism

Additional problems surfaced during the nineteenth and twentieth centuries as humanistic and naturalistic theories engulfed disciplines such as philosophy, psychology, sociology, literature, and science. This was the era of all-encompassing worldviews. Rationalistic systems of thought competed to capture the minds of men, and each one claimed itself to be true and all others false. This modern period eroded the Protestant respect for the Scriptures.

> "Post-modernism is modernism with the optimism taken out."
> — Robert Hewison, British Historian

Many university and seminary graduates who entered the pulpits of churches had been infected with ideas that were destructive to faith. They had begun to view God and religion as purely human creations, and the Bible as a patchwork of non-supernatural documents, a mosaic of myths and legends. Others managed to maintain a semblance of faith, but they developed doubts about the trustworthiness of the Scriptures. Yet the vast majority of evangelicals continued to hold the Scriptures in high esteem. From their ranks arose a number of truly conservative scholars who diligently prepared themselves both spiritually and academically to take the fight to the foe, having determined not to abandon the Bible to the enemy (1 Tim. 6:12). But their numbers were far too few to win the war.

Postmodernism

Two horrific world wars finished dampening the optimism of modernism, and it began to collapse. The "big pictures" proposed by rationalists lost credibility; perhaps, the biblical picture suffered most, as it was thought to be even less certain than the others. A new mindset called *postmodernism* had come into vogue, a worldview that considered all worldviews to be relative in nature. This popular postmodern mentality naturally displayed an anti-Christian and an anti-humanistic bias that continues into the present. Confidence has been lost in such things as the inductive method used in science, the rationalistic certainty of philosophy, the mechanistic regularity of the world, the upward progress of evolution, the subconscious world of psychoanalysis, and the classless society of communism. Postmodern feeling has replaced God, truth,

> Postmodern feeling has replaced God, truth, creation, and order with nothingness, relativism, chaos, and confusion. The result has been a crisis of meaning and the loss of hope.

reformatory movements in *A Manual of Church History* (American Baptist Publication Society, 1931), 2: 6-7.

creation, and order with nothingness, relativism, chaos, and confusion. The result has been a crisis of meaning and the loss of hope.[4]

The tremendous changes effected by modernism and postmodernism have helped greatly to marginalize the Bible in Western culture. Other factors have also contributed to its receding influence, especially religious pluralism. Religions other than Christianity have spread throughout Europe and America. Islamic and Buddhist shrines have risen in former evangelical strongholds. Globalization has made the Western world aware than many sacred texts other that the Bible are revered in most parts of the world. In addition, society's approval of alternative lifestyles—couples living as husband and wife outside marriage, homosexual orientation, same-sex marriage—has helped to increase distrust in Christian values as mandated in the New Testament. These formerly unaccepted forms of behavior are being approved more and more by a generation of liberally-minded Millennials. No longer are such hot-button issues much of a problem to them. Even greater threats than all of these changes in society are the ever-increasing enticement of materialism and the alarming distraction provided by technology. People seem to know and pursue everything except the Bible and its values.

Nulla Scriptura

Contemporary culture seems bent on removing the last vestiges of biblical authority and morality. Its battle-cry is "no Scripture" instead of "Scripture only." The liberal wing of Protestantism has already welcomed the lower view of the Bible. Quite alarming, however, is the downward spiral within some more conservative, evangelical segments of Protestantism.

The Evangelical Theological Society, founded in 1949 to promote conservative biblical scholarship, illustrates this point. Annually, its members must submit a signed affirmation that "the Bible alone in its entirety is the Word of God written and is therefore inerrant in the autographs." Within thirty years, however, some members had begun to express serious doubts about the statement.

The logo of Evangelical Theological Society Reads:
ΟΥ ΔΥΝΑΤΑΙ ΛΥΘΗΝΑΙ Η ΓΡΑΦΗ
"The Scriptures cannot be broken"
(John 10:35)

In 1983 one of the members was forced to resign from the Society because he published a commentary on Matthew that described the infancy narratives of Matthew as containing non-historical events as well as historical facts.[5] He argued Matthew was using a Jewish literary form (genre) called *midrash*. This view, however, was denounced as unorthodox.[6]

Today, more intensely than ever, the Bible's trustworthiness and integrity are being questioned.[7] One might hear, "We do not

---

[4] This paragraph is reworked from my lecture, "The Rise of Unbelief: Apologetics in Today's World," *A Place to Stand: Apologetics in an Uncertain Age* (Florida College Annual Lectures, 1999), 45.

[5] Robert H. Gundry, *Matthew: a Commentary on His Literary and Theological Art* (Eerdmans, 1982).

[6] Cf. Leslie R. Keylock, "Evangelical Scholars Remove Robert Gundry for His Views on Matthew," *Christianity Today*, Nov. 1, 2003.

[7] For example, read a number of the articles in the *Journal*

possess a single original manuscript of any book of the Bible; then, how can we affirm that the 'autographs' were 'inerrant' (free from error)?" Or, "A book like 2 Peter does not even belong in the Bible." And, "The phrase 'the Word of God' only applies to the oral word, not the written word." Finally, "The Holy Spirit still speaks to us today by means of those who possess charismatic gifts." Such statements are not intended to build confidence in the Scriptures and their all-sufficiency.

Conclusion

Don't be naïve. No one completely escapes the allurement of contemporary culture (1 Cor. 10:12). Reverence for the Scriptures is not learned from the world. A person who travels the highway of higher education will likely be tainted by negative viewpoints. Look to Jesus and follow Him in all things (Heb. 12:1-2). Remember also that faith comes by "hearing the word of God" (Rom. 10:17), not by what classroom professors teach or books about the Bible affirm (1 Cor. 2:11). The Scriptures must be allowed to sit in judgment on human hypotheses. Read what others say, whether they agree or not, but read critically and cautiously. Accept C. S. Lewis's advice to read at least one old book (preferably conservative) for every new one you read. Don't be deceived into thinking that new is better. That's "chronological snobbery."

MELVIN D. CURRY JR.

of the Evangelical Theological Society 57:1 (March 2014) and James Merrick and Stephen Garrett, editors. *Five Views of Biblical Inerrancy* (Zondervan, 2003).

Study Questions

1. What two doctrines did most leaders of the Protestant Reformation share in common?

   1) _____
   2) _____

   What were the Latin phrases that summarized these doctrines? _____
   _____

   Are both of these doctrines taught in Scripture (see Jas. 2:24; 2 Tim. 3:16-17)? _____
   _____
   _____

2. What were some differences in the way Martin Luther and John Calvin addressed issues of scriptural authority? _____
   _____
   _____

3. What was an unfortunate consequence of the so-called "Enlightenment" of the seventeenth and eighteenth centuries? _____
   _____
   _____

4. How did "Modernism" change the way the some viewed the Bible in the nineteenth and twentieth centuries? _____
   _____
   _____

5. In "Post-Modern" thought what has replaced God, truth, creation, and order? _____
   _____
   _____

   Have you met people like this? What do they beieve? _____
   _____
   _____

6. Historically, those who identify themselves as Evangelicals have affirmed a confidence in the inspiration, accuracy, and reliability of Scripture. What happened within the the Evangelical Theological Society in 1983 that shows changes in the thinking of some Evangelicals? _____
   _____
   _____

   Have you seen examples of denominationalists who place less emphasis or trust in Scripture? How was this manifested? _____
   _____
   _____
   _____

7. To whom does Hebrews 12:1-2 teach that Christians should look? _____
   _____

How does Romans 10:17 teach that faith comes? _____
_____
_____

Doe either of these texts teach us anything about how we should view Scripture in our lives and in our worship? If so, what? _____
_____
_____
_____
_____

Lesson 9

Empty Pews and Geographical Shifts:
The Decline of Mainline Protestant Denominations
By Ryan Boyer

When Martin Luther urged his German countrymen to greater obedience to what he understood the Bible to teach, he compared the word of God's grace to a "passing downpour" which first began in Israel, then passed to Greece, and Rome, but ultimately moved on when error and apostasy set in (Letter to the Town-Councilmen, *Luther's Works,* Vol. 10, 464). According to research done by the Pew Research Center, in 1910 66.3% of those who identified themselves as "Christians" lived in Europe. By 2010 this number had dropped to only about 25.9%.[1] A January 2015 story in the *Wall Street Journal* reported that hundreds of church buildings and cathedrals in Europe have closed their doors over the last decade because of dwindling memberships. Projections indicate that similar trends may be looming ahead in the United States. There are already nearly twice as many people in Sub-Saharan Africa (517,230,000) who identify themselves as "Christians" than in North America (266,630,000). Will the time come when brethren in Africa send men to the United States to help spread the gospel?

Mainline Protestantism has been in decline since the 1960s. The designation "mainline Protestant" describes the overwhelming majority of denominations in the United States in the 19th and first half of the 20th centuries which identify themselves as "Christian." While not limited to these, the big seven are the United Methodist Church, Evangelical Lutheran Church in America, Episcopal Church USA, Presbyterian Church USA, American Baptist Church, United Church of Christ, and The Christian Church (Disciples of Christ). Although these groups are still referred to as mainline, they are no longer the majority brand of denominationalism in the United States.

In addition to being the historical majority, theologically, mainline Churches are often contrasted with Evangelicals. The two main points of diversion for these classifications are (1) the nature of the Bible and (2) God's desire

[1] "Global Christianity – A Report on the Size and Distribution of the World's Christian Population" (*http://www.pewforum.org/2011/12/19/global-christianity-exec/*).

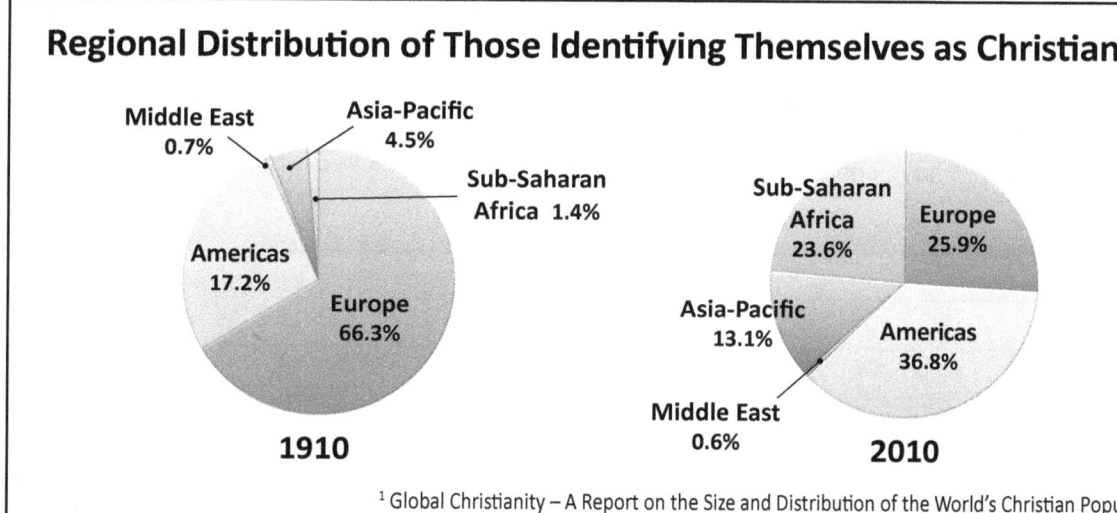

Regional Distribution of Those Identifying Themselves as Christians

1910 — Middle East 0.7%, Asia-Pacific 4.5%, Sub-Saharan Africa 1.4%, Americas 17.2%, Europe 66.3%

2010 — Sub-Saharan Africa 23.6%, Europe 25.9%, Asia-Pacific 13.1%, Americas 36.8%, Middle East 0.6%

[1] Global Christianity – A Report on the Size and Distribution of the World's Christian Population
http://www.pewforum.org/2011/12/19/global-christianity-exec/.

> Two main points of diversion between mainline churches and Evangelicals are 1) the nature of the Bible and 2) God's desire for humanity.

for humanity. First, mainline Protestants take a historical-critical approach to the Bible. The Bible, according to this method, is entirely of human origin and documents the historical and evolutionary development of Christian texts and theology. While Evangelicals disagree about the nature of inspiration, part of what makes one Evangelical is the conviction that the Bible is God's inspired word. Second, mainline Protestants view God's desire for Creation in terms of social justice. These groups have had roles in the civil rights movement, feminist agendas, in the political theater, and most recently, in the general acceptance and even clerical ordination of homosexuals. Due to this social justice element, African American denominations, such as the African Methodist Episcopal Church (AME), are considered mainline. Alternately, Evangelicals emphasize personal salvation (i.e. conversion and being born again) and the identification and eradication of sin as the central theme of God's plan.

Subjectively, it seems to me that the ideals of mainline Protestantism are flourishing. Objectively, however, in terms of overall membership, percentage of national population and number of congregations, mainline Protestantism has been in decline for more than half a century. William Weston said in 1992, "For a decade or so, the leaders and scholars of the old Protestant establishment have been trying to figure out what happened to the mainline churches. Spurred on by Robert Wood Lynn of the Lilly Endowment, a series of fine studies ... have charted the decline of the old mainline in the face of countless new religious movements and a rising conservative counter-establishment."[2] According to a 2008 Pew Forum *U.S. Religious Landscape Survey*, the United States was 18.1% mainline Protestant (not including 6.9% hist. black churches) and 26.3% Evangelical. Mainline is no longer synonymous with majority. Everybody acknowledges this reality, but the ten million dollar question is why? There is no end to explanations for this trend including demographic, geographical, and birth rate factors. I will offer TWO possible reasons for the reader's consideration.

First, when folks present the Bible as a product of human innovation and theological evolution there is only one inevitable dead end street at the end of that journey: The Bible is fallible, changeable, and ultimately pointless (cf. 1 Pet. 1:20-21; Acts 1:16). If I teach my kids that the Bible was invented by fallible men with no eternal significance, then why on earth should I be surprised when they no longer choose to participate? It is a self-defeating proposition. It is no wonder, then, that the primary venue of influence among mainline groups is within academia from those concerned more about history than religion. The alternative, that the Scriptures are the everlasting inspired word

---

[2] William J. Weston, Review of "The Mainstream Protestant Decline: The Presbyterian Pattern," ed. Milton J. Coalter, John M. Mulder, Louis B. Weeks. *Fides et Historia* 24:3 (Fall 1992): 143.

of God, not only gives ongoing purpose to one's being, but it is the reason why millions throughout history have chosen to commit their lives to the truths therein and to teach their children, brethren, family, neighbors, and friends to do the same. This subject needs to be regarded as foundationally critical in preaching and teaching in our homes. The Scriptures are from God and have eternal value (2 Tim. 3:16-17).

Second, it is not hard to imagine how the social gospel was born:

- The "spirit of the day" was one of social Darwinism and that humanity is ultimately perfectible.
- Nobody today would call the inhumane circumstances in the late 19th century, which were fueled by mass immigration, urbanization, industrialization, etc., acceptable.
- The ideals of Christianity lend themselves towards helping those less fortunate.

Eventually, however, a gospel founded upon making this world a better place is doomed to failure. Jesus taught, "the poor you will have with you always" (Matt. 26:11, NKJV). Jesus' Kingdom is not of this world. Jesus told Pilate, "my kingdom is not from the world" (John 18:36, ESV). Biblical Christianity presents a viably attainable goal that is not shattered in the face of World Wars, natural disasters, human suffering and things like these.

For the sake of future generations, we need to be crystal clear about who we are, where we belong, what we are doing and where we are going. Mainline Protestantism is reaping the fruits of their man-made religion as they continue to preach and teach members out of their pews.

RYAN BOYER

Study Questions

1. General labels, such as mainline and evangelical, frequently do not present a full and accurate picture of one's beliefs and practices. To illustrate some dangers of broadly labeling groups, research the following:

- The United Methodist Church (UMC) is the largest mainline denomination today. Theologically, however, are they generally considered mainline or evangelical? _____
_____
_____

- Not all Presbyterians are the same. Doctrinally and socially, which Presbyterian Church would be considered mainline and evangelical: Presbyterian Church USA (PCUSA), or Presbyterian Church in America (PCA)? _____
_____
_____
_____

- Not all Baptists are the same. Doctrinally and socially, which Baptist Church would be considered mainline and evangelical: American Baptist Church, or Southern Baptist Church? _____
_____
_____
_____

2. What do the following texts teach about the nature of the Bible: 2 Tim. 3:16-17; 2 Pet. 1:20-21; Acts 1:16; 4:24-25; Heb. 1:5-6? (NOTE: Consider the many times in the Bible the phrase, "Thus says the Lord…" is used.) _____
_____
_____
_____
_____

3. What are some long-term consequences of teaching that the Bible is ultimately a product of the human mind? _____
_____
_____

4. Conversely, what are some implications of regarding and teaching that the Scriptures originate with the Lord? _____
_____
_____
_____

5. Walter Rauschenbusch (1861-1918) is a key figure in the development of the social gospel movement. Consider these quotes as an introduction to some of his thinking: "Because the Kingdom of God has been dropped as the primary and comprehensive aim of Christianity, and personal salvation has been substituted for it, therefore men seek to save their own souls and are selfishly indifferent to the evangelization of the world."[3] The Kingdom of God, according to Rauschenbusch, "…is not a matter of getting individuals to heaven, but of transforming the life on earth into the harmony of heaven."

- What is the aim of Christianity according to the social gospel? _____

- What is the aim of Christianity according to the Bible (Ezek. 34:11-16; John 10:1-16; Luke 15:3-24)? _____

- What is the Kingdom of God according to the social gospel? _____

- What is the Kingdom of God according the Bible (Dan. 2:31-45; 7:9-14; Matt. 10:7; 12:28; Col. 1:13; Acts 28:28-30; 1 Cor. 6:9-10; 15:24, 50)? _____

- What does it mean to evangelize according to the social gospel? _____

- What does it mean to evangelize according to the Bible (Matt. 28:19-20; Acts 5:42)? _____

6. What are some long-term consequences of teaching that final purpose of God's plan for the world is to make this present world a better place? _____

7. Conversely, what are some implications of teaching that Jesus' kingdom is not of this world (John 18:36)? _____

Is an Impending Catholic – Protestant Convergence Coming?

By Curtis Pope

In a series of interviews conducted by David Holder and Coulter Wickerham of the former *Christianity Magazine* editors in 2009, Wickerham asked Dr. David Edwin Harrell a question concerning statements he had made about a future convergence of Catholics and Protestants.[1] While stating that such a convergence was probably still one hundred years in the future, Dr. Harrell reiterated his stand that the more denominational distinctions diminish, the more likely ultimate reunion would occur. While I am not a prophet, a son of a prophet, or even as well-read as Dr. Harrell, I tend to agree that within the time frame he mentions reunion is likely to occur, especially among mainline Protestant denominations and the Roman Catholic Church. I am less confident about a similar union of Evangelical Protestants and Sectarians with the Roman Church, mainly because it is hard for me to imagine that all of their denominational distinctions, especially their view of the Bible, would evaporate in such a relatively short period of time.

> The more that denominational distinctions diminish, the more likely it is that a reunion of Catholics and Protestants will occur.

The fact that Protestants and Catholics are finding more in common is obvious, however, to any objective observer. For about the last 250 years, Catholic and Protestant churches have been moving on two converging courses. First, mainline Protestant churches began to develop high church factions in the early nineteenth century. Then the study of source criticism, comparative religions, and the publication of Darwin's works had, by the time two-thirds of the nineteenth century had gone, produced a modernist philosophy that undermined the credibility and authority of the Bible and the uniqueness of Christianity. Catholicism, on the other hand, while more slowly adopting these trends, made an abrupt change in the 1960s by the conclusions of the Second Vatican Council. The result has been, by the early 21st century, denominations that are closer than they have ever been in their accepted doctrines and their views of ecumenicalism.

Pope Francis, Jorge Mario Bergoglio

While Catholic ecumenicalism has been slower to develop, its flourishing under Pope Francis was perfectly illustrated by a speech delivered by Thomas Rosica, President of the Catholic Assumption University in Windsor, Ontario, to the Committee of Ecumenical and Interreligious Affairs of the United States Conference of Catholic Bishops in November of 2014 and recorded in the February 23, 2015 issue of the Vatican Insider.[2] While pointing out ecumenical outreach to Eastern Orthodox, Evangelical, Pentecostal, Charismatic, and even Jewish groups, he illustrates the current pope's ecumenical efforts through homilies that were delivered by him over the last few years.

In the first of these on May 13, 2013, Pope Francis used as his text Paul's sermon on the Areopagus in Acts 17 indicating that Paul's effort was to build bridges rather to expound an "encyclopedia of truth." He also indicates that

---

[1] https://www.youtube.com/watch?v=6Xz94ExxSHk.

[2] http://vaticaninsider.lastampa.it/en/documents/detail/articolo/ecumenismo-ecumenism-ecumenismo-37469/.

Paul was seeking dialog and an encounter with truth, because "No one owns the truth."

In the second homily on October 13, 2013, he used as his text Luke 11:52. In this text Jesus condemns the teachers of the Law who have taken away the key of knowledge, preventing themselves and others from entering into a right relationship with God. He asserts that Jesus, by such a statement, is rejecting ideologies as always being rigid, frightening, chasing away and distancing people from the church, whereas the key of knowledge Jesus presents is tenderness, love, and meekness.

On October 24, 2014 a third homily uses 1 Peter 2:1-8 and its illustration of the church being made up of **"living stones."** He contrasts this with the disunity of the Tower of Babel constructed of bricks. He then asserts the point that virtues the world considers strong as stone are simply crumbling bricks, whereas the weaker virtues, such as humility, gentleness, and magnanimity, can develop us into strong stones. In fact, Paul, in Ephesians 4:1-3, emphasizes these weaker characteristics as preserving "the unity of the Spirit in the bond of peace" and deemphasizes the stone motif.

The final homily delivered by the pope on November 4, 2014 uses the story of the great dinner in Luke 14:16-24 to emphasize Jesus' effort to eventually compel (v. 23) all to come to the dinner. On the other hand, those initially invited who make excuses not to attend are described as selfish and afraid of God's "gratuity because they want it all for themselves." He concludes by asserting that it is difficult to listen to God's voice if all revolves around us.

This speech by Thomas Rosica, referencing Pope Francis's recent teachings, clearly illustrates the present pontiff's ecumenical emphasis, usually at the sacrifice of biblical context. This sacrifice, oddly enough, further indicates the growing similarity of modern Catholicism with mainline Protestantism by using Scripture as a springboard rather than a blueprint. It always serves as a problem when people use Scripture to justify their own agenda rather than allowing it to be the divine foundation upon which we build our belief and practice. The Lord does want unity among all true believers (John 17:21), but it must be based on a strict adherence to the New Testament as God's revealed Word. In fact, in John 17:17, in the same context in which unity is discussed, Jesus says, "Sanctify them in the truth; Your word is truth" (NASB). In John 10:4-5 Jesus emphasizes that his sheep "know His voice" and "they do not know the voice of strangers." Furthermore, such a lax attitude about Scripture leads to false practice, which Jesus describes in Matthew 15:9 as "vain worship." Therefore, any unity which disregards the authoritative nature of God's word is merely union.

As Dr. Harrell stated at the beginning of this article, within the next hundred years union is likely between Protestants and Catholics. While there may be exceptions to this, all signs point in that direction. But unlike the unity that Jesus desired and prayed for (John 17:21), it does not accomplish His will unless it is based upon His word. In Matthew 7:21 Jesus says, "Not everyone who says to Me, 'Lord, Lord,' will enter the kingdom of heaven, but he who does the will

> The Lord does want unity among all true believers (John 17:21), but it must be based on a strict adherence to the New Testament as God's revealed Word.

of My Father who is in heaven will enter." It takes more than mimicking the language of Scripture to be true disciples of the Lord, for in Matthew 15:13 Jesus clearly states that, "every plant which My heavenly Father did not plant shall be uprooted."

CURTIS POPE

Study Questions

1. In the homily (or sermon) given by Pope Francis on May 13, 2013, he argued that when Paul spoke before the Areopagus he was building bridges. Read Acts 17:16-34 and consider these questions:

    1) Did Paul teach any distinct and exclusive beliefs? If so, what? _____
    _____

    2) Did Paul's teaching call for change on the part of his hearers? _____
    _____

2. In the pope's homily on October 13, 2013 he asserts that Jesus' rebuke of the teachers of the Law taking away the "key of knowledge" is the Lord's rejection of strict ideology. Read Luke 11:52-53 and consider:

    1) What is meant by "entering in"? _____
    _____

    2) Does the Lord indicate that some do not "enter in"? Is this a "strict ideology"? _____
    _____

3. In the pope's homily on October 24, 2014 he compares "living stones" with the bricks of the Tower of Babel. Read 1 Peter 2:1-8 and consider these questions: 1) What are some other descriptions of those said to be "living stones" and what does the text say these people do? To whom is their action to be acceptable? _____
    _____

    Over what are some said to stumble in this text? Who or what is this, and why are people said to stumble over it? _____
    _____

4. The homily given by the pope on November 4, 2014 was on the parable of the great dinner. Read Luke 14:16-24 and consider: Were all people allowed to enjoy the dinner? Who was not and why? _____
    _____

5. In Jesus' prayer in John 17:17-21 what does Jesus pray may "sanctify" (or set apart) His people? ___
    _____

    In this prayer, what effect does Jesus indicate unity among believers will have on the world? _____
    _____

    Should the same thing that sets disciples apart make them one? _____
    _____

6. What does Matthew 7:21 indicate about a unity among believers that does not involve obedience and conformity to God's word? _____
_____
_____
_____

7. What does Matthew 15:13 indicaate about the fate of those holding to a faith not grounded in God's word? _____
_____
_____
_____

Lesson 11

"No One Comes to the Father Except through *Whom?*"

By Norman E. Sewell

There is a spirit of tolerance being pursued and urged upon us that seemingly calls upon us to accept the beliefs and actions of others regardless of how God views them. We see this in current attitudes toward sexual immorality. But tolerance is not the same as acceptance. This ecumenical spirit seeks to accept all who believe in one God, even those who do not call Jesus their Lord; and it asks that we regard all who claim to believe in Jesus as brothers. This spirit seeks to have all work together in a form of unity, yet it diminishes Jesus to merely a figurehead by ignoring His word. Where does this come from and where does it lead?

The logo of the World Council of Churches. The Greek word *oikomene* refers to the "inhabited world." The word *ecumenical* is derived from this word.

In 1948 a "world-wide inter-church organization was founded," and became the World Council of Churches (WCC). According to *Wikipedia* WCC describes itself as "a worldwide fellowship of 349 global, regional and sub-regional, national and local churches seeking unity, a common witness and Christian service." We find similar attempts in many local communities in their "ministerial alliances." In more recent days we find effort being made to bring various religions together. In 2008 King Abdullah of Saudi Arabia held a "World Conference on Dialogue" in Madrid, Spain. This dialogue included "representatives of Islam, Judaism, Christianity, Hinduism, Buddhism, Shintoism and Confucianism to reinforce the common values shared by their respective faiths." However, the king said, "God's will, praise be to Him, was that people should differ in their faiths. If the Almighty had so desired, all mankind would have shared the same religion" (Saudi Embassy news release from Madrid). While seeking some sort of dialogue, it is clear King Abdullah did not expect any real unity.

But this ecumenical spirit is closer than we thought. In January 2015 a "church of Christ" in Springfield, MO held a "Unity in Christ Worship" service. The announcement on their *Facebook* page told of their goal: "6 churches, one community of Christ's followers, one faith, one mission; lead people to Christ." The participants included a Methodist congregation, a Christian Church, a group called Hope Church, and apparently others. It was called a worship and prayer service, but the intent seems clear—to call others who claim faith in Jesus brothers and to work together with them in some kind of unity. So I have to ask, who is my brother? And, what constitutes unity in Christ?

What a blessing to be a child of God—His family! While we are all His offspring (Acts 17:28) and made in His image (Gen. 1:26-27), not all are His children, so not all are brothers. The criteria for being counted a child of God is not decided by man but by God Himself. John tells us that those who receive Jesus (i.e., believe in Him) have the "RIGHT TO BECOME children of God," to be "born of God" (John 1:11-13, emphasis mine). Jesus describes this process as a new birth, being born "of water and the Spir**it**" (John 3:5). And Paul shows us that this includes putting on Christ in baptism, thus becoming heirs of God's promise (Gal. 3:26-29). No person outside of Christ can be my brother using God's standard.

Salvation and eternal life are clearly in Christ. As Jesus prepared the disciples for His death He responded to Thomas by saying, "I am the way, the Truth, and the life. No one comes to the Father except

> How then can unity be obtained? Unity can only be achieved when all are agreed on the same standard; when all questions are answered from one source of authority.

through Me" (John 14:6). Concerning Jesus, Peter said, "Nor is there salvation in any other, for there is no other name under heaven given among men by which we must be saved" (Acts 4:12). Further, He (i.e., Jesus) is the "author of eternal salvation to all who obey Him" (Heb. 5:9); and the "author and finisher of our faith" (Heb. 12:2). Jesus' prayer was for unity, that all believers would be one, as He and the Father are one (John 17:20-21).

How then can unity be obtained? Unity can only be achieved when all are agreed on the same standard; when all questions are answered from one source of authority. Jesus asked the chief priests and elders if John's baptism was "from heaven or from men" (Matt. 21:25). Paul called upon the Ephesian Christians to "keep the unity of the Spirit in the bond of peace" (Eph. 4:3). If we can't agree on "one body and one Spirit, just as you were called in one hope of your calling; one Lord, one faith, one baptism; one God and Father of all" (Eph. 4:4-6), how will we ever be united?

We must exhibit a spirit of humility realizing our imperfections, seeking to "be likeminded, having the same love, being of one accord, of one mind," and giving up all selfishness to have the mind of Christ (Phil. 2:2-5). Should we show tolerance of the beliefs and conscience of others? Yes! Acceptance of things not approved by God? NO!

NORMAN E. SEWELL

Study Questions

Concerning God's Family:

1. Can you be in God's family without Jesus (John 1:11-13; 14:6)? _____

    a. Can I have eternal life without Him (1 John 5:11-12)? _____

2. Can I be part of the family without being born again (John 3:5-7)? _____

3. How do I put on Christ (Gal. 3:26-27)? _____

    a. Have you put Him on? _____

Concerning Unity:

1. Who would be "one" in Jesus' prayer for unity (John 17:20-21)? _____

2. Is unity even possible (Eph. 4:3-6; Phil. 2:2-5)? _____

3. If a thing is not "from heaven" where is it from (Matt. 21:25)? _____

Conservative Thinking within the Denominational World

By Jeff Wilson

The religious world of the nineteenth century produced some contrasting extremes. The Darwinian evolutionary thinking applied to religious studies by men like Julius Wellhausen produced the so-called "Documentary Hypothesis." This theory that the Pentateuch was the product of documents cut and pasted together, set the stage for a widespread rejection of a belief in the inspiration of Scripture in much of the religious world in the twentieth century. On the other extreme, men such as Barton W. Stone, Thomas, and Alexander Campbell, and others like them were equally entrenched in the denominational world of this same century. These men, however, did not move away from a trust in the authority of God's word, but toward a greater respect for it as the absolute authority in matters of faith and practice. What influenced such extremes? Are similar dynamics at work in our day? Are there men and women of "an honest and good heart" (Luke 8:15, NASB), presently in error who are poised for similar moves toward a greater respect and obedience to God's word? How can Christians identify such souls, and influence them for good?

Julius Wellhausen

Thomas Campbell

The Problem

There is a perennial temptation to isolate ourselves from denominational influences by cutting ourselves off from any contact with them, including reading any books, articles, or other materials that are produced by the denominational or academic worlds. The reticence to read such items is understandable given the immense potential for being led astray by authors who are learned and eloquent, yet also captive to various unscriptural errors. Scripture indeed teaches, "do not participate in the unfruitful deeds of darkness, but instead even expose them" (Eph. 5:11).

Yet a principled, absolute abandonment of reading any works other than those produced by brethren or seeking any opportunity for influence and understanding has its own inherent risks. C. S. Lewis, in his classic essay "On the Reading of Old Books," efficiently explains the danger in reading only new books (because they are presumably up-to-date and therefore better) as compared to old books. He wrote:

> Every age has its own outlook. It is specially good at seeing certain truths and specially liable to make certain mistakes. We all, therefore, need books that will correct the characteristic mistakes of our own period.

His basic point, as it pertains to historical understanding, is equally applicable in studying the Bible. Everyone is liable to be blind to certain flaws and unaware of that blindness. Just as books from other eras can correct modern blindness to our own flaws, so too can books from outside our fellowship show us things about the Bible or ourselves that we may not have noticed.

A Possible Solution: Plunder the Egyptians

All truth is God's truth. Just because a denominational preacher or scholar is in error with regards to some of his teaching, does it necessarily follow that he is in error in all that he says or writes?

As an ancient analogy to our contemporary consideration of this issue, those attempting to be Christians in the earliest centuries struggled with whether or not Christians should read or study pagan works (Homer, Plato, Aristotle, Virgil, etc.). While Tertullian famously and memorably thought not, asking the question, "What has Athens to do with Jerusalem?" (*On the Prescription of Heretics* 7), Augustine had a more nuanced and, ironically, biblical approach. Specifically, Augustine wrote that Christians should follow ancient Israel's example and "plunder the Egyptians" (cf. Exod. 3:19-22; 12:36). He wrote:

> Moreover, if those who are called philosophers ... have said aught that is true and in harmony with our faith, we are not only not to shrink from it, but to claim it for our own use from those who have unlawful possession of it. For, as the Egyptians had not only the idols and heavy burdens which the people of Israel hated and fled from, but also vessels and ornaments of gold and silver, and garments, which the same people when going out of Egypt appropriated to themselves, designing them for a better use, not only doing this on their own authority, but by the command of God, the Egyptians themselves, in their ignorance, providing them with things which they themselves were not making a good use of; in the same way all branches of heathen learning have not only false and superstitious fancies ... but they contain also liberal instruction which is better adapted to the use of the truth, and some most excellent precepts of morality; and some truths in regard even to the worship of the One God are found among them.... These, therefore, the Christian, when he separates himself in spirit from the miserable fellowship of these men, ought to take away from them, and to devote to their proper use in preaching the gospel (*On Christian Doctrine* II.60).

We wouldn't agree with Augustine that pagan philosophers teach us about "the worship of the One God," unless he means that even pagans recognize the reality of a Creator to whom reverence is due (cf. Rom. 1:18-21). Even so, his comparison of Israel's plunder of the Egyptians in application to our attitude toward valuable things in the possession of those outside of Christ is compelling.

Perhaps we can extend Augustine's point even further—if even pagans sometimes correctly perceive and write things that are at least in part true, how much can we potentially find useful observations and points from select denominational writers who (while most definitely in error on some points and particulars), are also (if we are honest about it), at least in some cases sincerely seeking the same thing we are? There are now, and always have been, those outside God's fellowship to whom it could be said as Jesus once said to an ancient Scripture scholar "you are not far from the kingdom of God" (Mark 12:34). Will we even know about such souls if we are unwilling to look for them? Can inquiry into such resources open opportunities for us to influence those around us of a similar mindset?

> There are now, and always have been, those outside God's fellowship to whom it could be said as Jesus once said to an ancient Scripture scholar "you are not far from the kingdom of God" (Mark 12:34).

This is all well and good, but most importantly of all, can we bring the Bible itself even more specifically to bear on this issue? I believe we can.

The apostle Paul was a well-educated man in his own time and place, as is made clear both in his own self description (Acts 22:3), as well as by his reputation (Acts 26:24). Paul was equally at

View of the ruins of the agora (or marketplace) of ancient Athens showing the Areopagus (or "Mars Hill") on the bottom left.

home with the depths of Jewish learning as well as the breadth of Greco-Roman culture. Is it possible that Paul's educational background may have been part of what made him God's fit chosen vessel to take the gospel to the Gentiles? Here was a man thoroughly versed in the Old Testament Scriptures that pointed to Christ while equally equipped to communicate that truth in ways that would resonate within the mainstream culture of the Greco-Roman world. Does this offer a model for us?

Indeed, it was Paul whom God providentially sent to Athens, the intellectual capital of the ancient world, to deliver for the first time to that city God's good news. And it was there that Paul did this divine work by connecting something that *"one of your own poets"* had gotten right with the gospel of Jesus Christ. In Acts 17:28, Paul quotes from Aratus' *Phaenomena* ("For we also are His offspring"). Titus 1:12 shows Paul citing another pagan—traditionally considered to be Epimenides ("Cretans are always liars, evil beasts, lazy gluttons")—even going so far as to note that the pagan was correct! In 1 Timothy 6:10 Paul says that "the love of money is the root of all kinds of evil," a general observation made by a number of ancient writers (traditionally including Diogenes of Sinope). Then there is 1 Corinthians 15:33 where Paul cites Menander ("Bad company corrupts good morals"). Clearly, it is the Holy Spirit that led Paul to make these citations, but it demonstrates that even inspired writers do not shun truth simply because one who is in error and unbelief may be the one who voiced it.

Caveats and Warnings

But by no means should I be construed as saying that brethren *en masse* should then read widely and indiscriminately in the larger religious world's literature. Those who are not well-grounded in Scripture must first become well "nourished on the words of the faith and of the sound doctrine" (1 Tim. 4:6). Only then will we be able to "to discern between the unclean and the clean" (Ezek. 44:23). Yet, even when we have done that several caveats are in order.

1. Filtering and Use. The apostle's example reminds us that what we do read and learn in the larger culture around us must always first be filtered through the gospel as God's truth and must also be put to use for God's kingdom purposes. Paul taught, "examine everything carefully; hold fast to that which is good" (1 Thess. 5:21).

2. Guarding and Sifting. Whenever we read denominational works, we need to be extremely careful to guard our minds as we read. This is equally true when making contact with those we

> Whenever we read denominational works, we need to be extremely careful to guard our minds as we read.

seek to influence. The goal is to sift the wheat from the chaff in these sorts of works, and find the sincere seeking souls we hope to influence, but carelessness in handling these works or in talking with those in the denominational world can lead to confusion in our own hearts and minds.

3. Reason and Purpose. There should be a selectiveness and intentionality in what works we choose to read and use. Don't be distracted by the religious bookstore's bestseller list or tempted to economize at the discount bin. Have a reason and a purpose for the denominational literature that you choose to use. Consider, as you make your reading choices, how this can help you help others.

A Strategy for Reading Denominational Scholarship

The reality is that we already interact with denominational scholarship by virtue of the fact that the very Bible translations we depend upon are all products of the denominational world. To put it another way: all of the reputable translations brethren use—King James Version and New King James Version, American Standard and New American Standard Version, even the more recent English Standard Version—are all productions of denominational scholars. But this observation leads to what may well be the most significant treasure we can "plunder from the Egyptians."

The fact that already our most frequent encounter with denominational Biblical scholarship is through our translations themselves demonstrates where denominational scholars can be extremely beneficial to us: in helping us better understand the Biblical text itself. All of the modern translations I just referenced above (ASV, NASB, ESV) are highly literal translations produced by scholars who take the Bible seriously and authoritatively. Although we would differ with many of them on matters of salvation and the work of the church, their attitude toward the inerrancy of Scripture is very conservative. This underscores the fact that there are many scholars among the Evangelicals as well as a few even among the mainline denominations whose books, articles, and

Five Major Formal Equivalence (or Literal) Translations

King Janes Version
1611 (Revised 1873)
Committee of Scholars
Authorized Version (AV)

American Standard Version
1901 American
Revision Committee

New American Standard Bible
1971 (Updated 1995)
Lockman Foundation

New King James Version
1982
Thomas Nelson Publishers

English Standard Version
2001
Crossway Bibles

NOTES

commentaries can help us understand the deeper significance of aspects of the Hebrew, Aramaic, or Greek original text that cannot be communicated in literal translation. These might include aspects of ancient history or culture that enlighten our understanding of the Biblical text and thus enhance our ability to hear all the more the nuance and depth of God's revelation to us. Such writers can help us see the literary character of the original text allowing us to better understand the full-scale context of various stories or teachings. While the cautions mentioned above apply equally to the use of scholarly works, Christians can benefit from the careful use of conservative scholarship.

Opportunities for Influence

The error and apostasy of our day certainly provides reason for concern. Many in the religious world have moved further and further away from biblical patterns. At the same time, as in the nineteenth century (and all generations) there are souls presently caught up in error, yet with hearts **"not far from the kingdom of God"** (Mark 12:34). May we seek them out, understand their views, and work to lead them out of error and to the truth, (cf. 2 Tim 2:24-26).

JEFF WILSON

Study Questions

1. What attitudes do you believe influence whether a denominational person moves away from obedience to the word of God, or closer to a sound understanding of what God demands of us? _____
   _____
   _____
   _____

2. If you have never done so, read the translation committee's preface at the front of the Bible version that you use. What do you learn about the nature of Bible translation in general and the people who produced your translation in particular? _____
   _____
   _____

   a. What questions does the preface raise in your mind that you need to study further? _____
   _____
   _____

3. Part of wise and mature Christian living is that we continually examine ourselves (2 Cor. 13:15). What particular spiritual dangers might using denominational study aids pose to your own spiritual well-being? _____
   _____
   _____

   a. Are you well-enough grounded in Scripture's truth to avoid being led astray by such works? _____
   _____
   _____
   _____

4. When seeking to influence someone in the religious world who demonstrates good attitudes toward the world of God, what are some good ways to help them move closer to full obedience to the gospel? __
   _____
   _____
   _____

   a. How can we exercise caution when working with such a person not to be influenced by errroneous views they might still hold? _____
   _____
   _____
   _____

5. Thinking through the issues raised in this essay, are there any denominational works in your own personal library that have had a spiritually dangerous effect on you? _____
   _____
   _____
   _____
   _____

   a. Are there books that you perhaps ought to remove from your personal library? _____
   _____
   _____

Is It Still Possible to be Simply Christians?

By Kyle Pope

Lesson 13

When Jesus came to this earth, He declared His intention to build His church (Matt. 16:18). The New Testament identified this church as His body (Eph. 1:22-23), and declared there is only "one body" (Eph. 4:4). In spite of these clear teachings, many in modern times deny that it is still even possible to be what Christians were in the New Testament. Is the goal of being simply Christians without any denominational affiliation still even possible, or must Christians concede to some unavoidable denominational identification?

Some Important Questions

To answer this question we must first ask ourselves a few other very important questions.

1. *Are Christians commanded to be united?* Yes. Paul commanded the Corinthians, "that you all speak the same thing, and that there be no divisions among you, but that you be perfectly joined together in the same mind and in the same judgment" (1 Cor. 1:10). This is a condition toward which Christians must aspire.

Ruins of Ancient Caesarea Philippi Jesus was "in the region of Caesarea Philippi" (Matt. 16:13) when He declared His intention to build His church (Matt. 16:18).

2. *Does God ever command things that are impossible for us to do?* No, God never expects anything from us that we are incapable of doing. When God gave the Law to Israel, He made it clear that the commandment of the Law was "not too mysterious for you, nor is it far off" (Deut. 30:11)—it was near and accessible "that you may do it" (Deut. 30:14). The same is true of the Law of Christ (cf. 1 Cor. 10:13). So, if we are commanded to be united, we must conclude that it is possible to be united in doctrine and practice.

3. *Is God pleased with Christians being divided in doctrine and practice?* No. Jesus prayed that His disciples might be one (John 17:21), but He also warned them not to turn aside to false teaching (Matt. 7:15-20). We must conclude that it is God's will that His disciples remain united in faith and practice and to do otherwise is to act contrary to God's will and in a manner displeasing to Him.

4. *Can Christians depart from sound doctrine and still remain a part of Christ's body?* No. Jesus warned individuals that those who do not bear fruit will be cut off from Him (John 15:5-6). Jesus also warned churches unwilling to repent that they would be removed from His presence (Rev. 2:5). If an individual, therefore, departs from following the word of God, he or she does not remain a part of Christ's body. John taught, "Whoever transgresses and does not abide in the doctrine of Christ does not have God. He who abides in the doctrine of Christ has both the Father and the Son" (2 John 9). Groups of individuals who have departed from following God's word cannot, therefore, be representative of sound congregations of those who are a part of the Lord's church.

5. *Is it ever necessary for Christians to separate themselves from those in error?* Yes. The church is to withdraw from one who refuses

> Jesus prayed that His disciples might be one (John 17:21), but He also warned them not to turn aside to false teaching (Matt. 7:15-20).

to repent when rebuked for sin (Matt. 18:15-17). Withdrawal from the unrepentant is aimed at the restoration of one in error (1 Cor. 5:5) and to keep the church sound (1 Cor. 5:6-8). An unrepentant Christian from whom the church has withdrawn may still be considered a brother (2 Thess. 3:15), but he or she is not in an acceptable relationship with God. Christians must not "keep company with him that he may be ashamed" (2 Thess. 3:14). Those who have never come to Christ cannot be counted as brethren. We may seek to teach such a person (cf. Acts 18:24-26; 19:1-5), but one who expresses tolerance and acceptance of that which is outside of the doctrine of Christ "shares in his evil deeds" (2 John 10).

Confronting the Reality of Division

In spite of all of these clear teachings in Scripture, it is clear that division exists among those who call themselves Christians. Let's consider a few questions about this:

1. Does simply calling oneself a "Christian" truly identify him or her as a Christian? No. Jesus said there would be those who would call Him "Lord" and yet by refusing to do His will be denied as His disciple on the Day of Judgment (Matt. 7:21-23). It is the Bible, not human beings, that defines who is and is not a Christian, or disciple of Christ (cf. Acts 11:26).

2. What determines whether an individual or group truly belongs to Christ? Jesus said that abiding in His word determines if one is or is not His disciple (John 8:31). We must conclude, therefore, that if a group calls itself a part of Christ and yet does not teach and practice what is taught in the Bible, such a group cannot truly be said to be a part of Christ.

3. What is a "denomination"? We can understand how to define a denomination by considering the etymology of the word itself. In Latin the word *nomen* meant, "name." This came into English in our word *nominate*, which means literally to "name" a person for a task or office. The prefix *de-* when added to this word, either intensifies the primary meaning, or adds the sense of "away" from the thing *named*. To *denominate* something is to distinguish it in name from something else. Two things of a different "denomination" are not the same thing in nature or quality. A penny is not a nickel—a dime is not a quarter, etc.

The Bible never uses the word "denomination," but in English the dictionary defines a denomination as "a recognized autonomous branch of the Christian Church" (*New Oxford American Dictionary*). This very definition shows the unscriptural nature of this concept. Jesus told His disciples, "I am the vine, you are the branches" (John 15:5). The "branches" of the Lord's church are individual disciples. An individual is either part of Christ or outside of Christ. To be *autonomous* is "acting independently or having the freedom to do so" (*New Oxford American Dictionary*). An individual cannot be autonomous. Paul declared, "I have been crucified with Christ; it is no longer I who live, but Christ lives in me" (Gal. 2:20). Individuals have freewill, but we cannot act independently of Christ. Paul taught that Christians have become "slaves of God" (Rom. 6:22). In the same way, groups of people are either part of Christ or outside of Christ. If they are a part of Christ they

Organization of the Lord's Church

The Church Universal

Christ is the Head
Ephesian 1:22; Colossians 1:18

The Church in Submission to Him
Ephesian 5:24

AUTONOMOUS CONGREGATIONS

No pope. No headquarters. No convention.

The Local Church

ELDERS

Qualifications:
1 Timothy 3:1-13
Titus 1:5-9

Also Called:
Bishops, Overseers, Shepherds, Presbyters
1 Peter 5:1-3

Members in Submission
Hebrews 13:17

DEACONS   INDIVIDUAL CHRISTIANS

Leading a congregation by the word of God – Titus 1:9

---

are the same in nature and identity. When Jesus taught His disciples not to elevate disciples one over another, He explained, "you are all brethren" (Matt. 23:8). We cannot *denominate* something from another thing and yet say it is the same in identity and nature.

We can speak of local congregations as autonomous, but that refers to issues of leadership. The New Testament teaches no church government higher than the eldership of local congregations (Acts 14:23) and yet lower than the headship of Christ (Eph. 5:23). One eldership does not rule over another church. In this sense congregations are autonomous, but even congregations must be in submission to the headship of Christ (Eph. 5:24). If two congregations are different and distinct in practice or teaching, one (or both) is either obedient to God's word or in rebellion to God's word. So, the individuals who are a part of that group are not, therefore, part of the church that belongs to Christ.

4. *Is biblical unity accomplished by accepting unity in diversity?* No. Paul taught the same things "everywhere in every church" (1 Cor. 4:17). The Bible teaches patience and respect for conscience (Rom. 15:1), but it also warns that one may "condemn himself" by approving of that which is wrong (Rom. 14:22). Christians are taught to oppose apostasy. Paul commanded the Romans, "Now I urge you, brethren, note those who cause divisions and offenses, contrary to the doctrine which you learned, and avoid them" (Rom. 16:17). On a personal level brethren are to bear with one another, teach one another, and be patient with one another, but that must never involve tolerance of sin or endorsement of error.

There are clearly matters of judgment in which congregations have the liberty to choose different ways to fulfill the Lord's commands. For example, while the church is commanded to *sing* or *speak to one another* in "psalms and hymns and spiritual songs, singing and making melody

NOTES

> If congregations differ in matters of judgment it does not compromise their unity or their obedience to the word of God—they are still fulfilling the Lord's instructions.

in your heart to the Lord" (Eph. 5:19; cf. Col. 3:16), we are not told how many songs, or what order in which those songs must fall during a time of worship. We are not told whether the songs are to be in four-part harmony, or whether a congregation is to sing from a printed songbook or from a projection of the words and music. If congregations differ in these matters of judgment it does not compromise their unity or their obedience to the word of God—they are still fulfilling the Lord's instruction to *sing* or *speak to one another* in song.

On the other hand if a congregation decides to add a mechanical instrument into their song worship the members of that congregation are adding an activity to this instruction that the Lord has not commanded. *To sing* or *speak* is not the same activity as *playing* an instrument. The words of Scripture do not authorize this addition. It is therefore a departure from Scripture that compromises abiding in the word of Christ (and therefore compromises unity between brethren). On a personal level faithful Christians may try to work with, teach, and persuade a brother or sister who improperly approves of this addition, but if this unauthorized act is compelled upon a group of Christians it must be opposed and rejected. If a group refuses to end this unscriptural act, a faithful Christian must remove himself from identification with such a congregation.

Can We Still Be Simply Christians?

We have attempted to logically and in an orderly fashion consider the issues pertinent to this question. After doing so, we can answer emphatically, *yes we can still be nothing more and nothing less than what Christians were in the New Testament!* Let us end by considering what this question really means. Sadly, even among brethren who once championed the call to be "Christians only" more and more from within our own ranks concede to the terminology of the world. What are we really saying if we do that? What are the logical consequences of taking such a position?

On one extreme, if it is not possible to be simply what Christians were in the New Testament then we cannot identify ourselves as "simply Christians." Instead, we must be "Stone-Campbell Christians" or part of the "Church of Christ" denomination. The Bible condemns party names whether those names represent respected brothers in Christ or not (1 Cor. 3:4). Further, the term "churches of Christ" (Rom. 16:16) is used in Scripture of congregations of the Lord's people who are in a saved relationship with Him, but never of some segment of the church universal that is a subset of the body of Christ.

On the other extreme, if it is not possible to be simply Christians without some denominational allegiance, we must accept that one can abide in Christ while failing to abide in His word! Are denominations following the word of God? No. They are divided in doctrine and practice and have adopted things that are outside of the word of Christ. As we saw above, by definition a disciple of Christ abides in His word (John 8:31). One cannot have a relationship with God while stepping outside of the doctrine of Christ (2 John 9). If I can be a Christian in a denomination then I am saying I can be a disciple while refusing to abide in the word of Christ.

NOTES

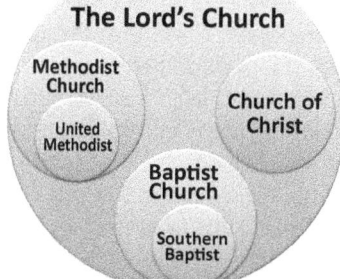

"The churches of Christ greet you" (Romans 16:16)

Scriptural Use — The Lord's Church (Church in Rome, Church in Corinth, Church in Jerusalem). All were "churches of Christ." Individuals in a saved relationship with God constitute the Lord's church universally.

Unscriptural Use — The Lord's Church (Methodist Church, United Methodist, Baptist Church, Southern Baptist, Church of Christ). The Baptist Church is not the Methodist Church. The Methodist Church is not the Church of Christ.

"What about Grace?"

Someone might say at this point—*"But, what about grace?"* It is clear that our salvation is not accomplished by our meritorious, and flawless ability to follow the Law of Christ, but by the merciful willingness of God to forgive our sin by His grace through the shed blood of Jesus Christ (Eph. 2:8). All souls fall short of God's glory (Rom. 3:23), and "all those things which you are commanded" are simply "what was our duty to do" (Luke 17:10). So, even when we do what we should we still need God's grace!

We must note, however, some important facts about the grace of God. *Is it universal and automatic?* No. The soul outside of Christ will die in sin (John 8:24), and be condemned to hell. Paul said, "Through HIM [i.e. Jesus] we have received grace" (Rom. 1:5, emphasis mine). If one has not *put on* Christ in obedience to the gospel (Gal. 3:27), he or she is not yet a recipient of "the grace of God that brings salvation" (Titus 2:11).

Someone might then say, *"But what about those folks that are so close?"* The Bible does speak of those who are "not far from the kingdom of God" (Mark 12:34), but being *close* to the kingdom is not the same thing as being *in* or *a part of* the kingdom. Notice this in the example of Apollos. When Aquila and Priscilla learned that Apollos "spoke and taught accurately the things of the Lord" and yet "he knew only the baptism of John" (Acts 18:25), they did not say "Oh, you're a *John the Baptist Christian*—Let's be in

> If one has not put on Christ in obedience to the gospel (Gal. 3:27), he or she is not yet a recipient of "the grace of God that brings salvation" (Titus 2:11).

unity, brother!" Scripture tells us, "they took him aside and explained to him the way of God more accurately" (Acts 18:26). We can appreciate those we may meet in the denominational world who have a respect for God's word and are close in their understanding of many things. But if we fail to *explain to them the way of God more accurately* or somehow communicate to them that they are acceptable before God in a condition in which they do not abide in the word of Christ we are contradicting the word of God! Our task is to be "good stewards of the manifold grace of God" (1 Pet. 4:10), not to put ourselves in the place of God passing judgments He has not revealed!

KYLE POPE

Study Questions

1. If the Bible teaches that Jesus established only one church (Matt. 16:18; Eph. 4:4), why do you think some people think a person has to be a member of a denomination and not simply a Christian? ____
   _____
   _____
   _____

2. Are Christians commanded to be united (1 Cor. 1:10)? _____
   _____

   Is God pleased with a religious world that is divided (John 17:21)? _____
   _____

   Is there ever a time when it is necessary to separate (Matt. 18:15-17; 1 Cor. 5:5-8; 2 Thess. 3:14-15; 2 John 9-10)? Why or why not? _____
   _____
   _____
   _____

3. Why do these churches avoid "traditional doctrines" such as the need for baptism, the significance of the Lord's Supper, or the roll of women in public worship? _____
   _____
   _____

4. What determines if a person truly belongs to Christ (John 8:31)? _____
   _____

5. What is the meaning of the Latin word *nomen*? _____
   _____

   What does the English word "nominate" literally mean? _____
   _____

   If we "denominate" something from another thing, do we still consider it to be the same thing in name or nature? _____
   _____

6. How can we show from the dictionary definition of the word "denomination" that it is an unscriptural concept? _____
   _____
   _____
   _____

7. In John 15:5 whom does Jesus identify as the "branches"? _____
   _____
   _____

   Are these denominations? Why or why not? _____
   _____
   _____

8. What does Romans 16:17 teach that runs counter to the concept of unity in diversity? _____
_____
_____
_____

9. How does diversity in matters of judgment differ from diversity over things taught in Scripture? _____
_____
_____
_____

10. Is the name "Church of Christ" used in Scripture as the name of a denomination (Rom. 16:16)? How is it used? _____
_____
_____
_____

11. In Luke 17:10 what does Jesus say we have done when we have done all things we are commanded to do? _____
_____

Does this merit salvation? Is it expected in order to receive grace? _____
_____
_____

12. Who does Scripture teach will receive God's grace unto salvation (see John 8:24; Rom. 1:5; Gal. 3:26-27; Titus 2:11)? _____
_____
_____
_____

If one stands outside of Christ can he or she expect to receive God's grace unto salvation? _____
_____
_____

If denominations do not teach what the Scripture requires to bring one into fellowship with Christ can they expect to receive God's grace unto salvation? Why or why not? _____
_____
_____
_____
_____

13. What does the example of Apollos in Acts 18:25-26 teach us about how to respond to those who are close in their understanding of scriptural principles? _____
_____
_____
_____
_____

Appendix

Faith in Faith vs. Faith in God

By Mike Willis

This title may sound a bit confusing and its relevance to "The Changing Face of Denominationalism" theme may not be immediately apparent, but the concept that is being examined is a serious threat to Christianity in the twenty-first century.

The situation is this: Twenty-first century Christianity (in the broadest sense of the term) does not believe that it makes any difference what one believes so long as one believes. Twenty-first century Americans frequently have a smorgasbord approach to religion that views choosing what religious beliefs one accepts to be somewhat like going through a cafeteria line and choosing what dishes he wishes to put on his plate for dinner. If there is something offered that one does not want, such as spinach salad or broiled flounder, he simply passes by those things and chooses for himself jello salad and strawberry pie. The result of this view of the Christian faith is that faith is not defined by the content of Scripture (as the Bible teaches that it should be) or by the affirmations of one's denominational creed or the teachings of the local church (as has been practiced by many Christian denominations), but by the individual's personal preference. Every man defines and creates his own personal faith. Since there are about 320 million people in the United States, there are about 320 million different religions in America.

In this concept of faith, the saving efficiency of faith is not defined by its object (God) or content (what is believed) but by the individual's choice to believe it, to commit himself to that belief system. So, an individual has faith in the power of faith rather than faith in God who has revealed Himself to mankind. And ironically, since the saving act is believing and not its object or contents, the more irrational the faith, the more commitment it takes to believe, so the greatest believer must be the one who believes the most irrational things – e.g., the moon is made out of blue cheese!

In the New Testament, the apostles and disciples of Christ were sent into the world to preach the gospel to all of mankind. Mark replicated Jesus' words as follows: "Go into all the world and preach the gospel to every creature. He who believes and is baptized will be saved; but he who does not believe will be condemned" (Mark 16:15-16). Let us keep in mind the historical situation in which this commission was given. First, the gospel was to be taken first to the Jews. The Jews already believed in Yahweh/Jehovah, accepted the Old Testament as the inspired word of God, and tried to live by the moral requirements taught therein. Yet, one could die a Jew without being saved by the shed blood of Jesus Christ, despite his faith – his mental assent and personal devotion to the things taught in the Old Testament. So said Jesus to a Jewish audience in these words: "Therefore I said to you that you will die in your sins; for if you do not believe that I am He, you will die in your sins" (John 8:24). Again, He said, "I am the way, the truth, and the life. No one comes to the Father except through Me" (John 14:6). The disciples heard this message from Jesus and spoke to their Jewish audience after Jesus' resurrection to heaven saying, "Nor is there salvation in any other, for there is no other name under heaven given among men by which we must be saved" (Acts 4:12). Salvation is contingent on what one believes about God's saving grace through the death of His Son.

Second, the gospel was taken to Gentiles, who themselves were also believers. Their beliefs and objects of devotion were varied, but they were believers nonetheless. The Gentile audience in Ephesus was quite committed to faith in Diana, as was all of the province of Asia. This Ephesian audience composed of Gentiles understood correctly that Paul "persuaded and turned away many people, saying that they are not gods which are made with hands" (Acts 19:26). The people of Athen worshiped many deities. Their beliefs are alluded to in Luke's account of Paul's sermon: "Men of Athens, I perceive that in all things you are very religious; for as I was passing through and considering the objects of your worship, I even found an altar with this inscription: TO THE UNKNOWN GOD. Therefore, the One whom you worship without knowing, Him I proclaim to you" (Acts 17:22). The purpose of preaching the gospel to Gentiles is expressed by Paul in his letter to the Thessalonians: "For they themselves declare concerning us what manner of entry we had to you, and how you *turned to God from idols to serve the living and true God*, and to wait for His Son from heaven, whom He raised from the dead, even Jesus who delivers us from the wrath to come" (1 Thess. 1:9-10).

The biblical narrative of preaching to both Jews and Gentiles makes no sense if the mere act of believing is salvific, if it makes no difference what one believes, just so long as he believes. If all that is necessary is the act of believing then the Jewish believers and the Gentiles believers were already saved despite the disparity in what they believed. Why was there a need to labor so arduously and endure such persecutions as these early disciples went through if one is able to be saved by the act of believing, without regard to its content?

The fact is that faith must be in God; there is no saving power in the mere act of believing! God revealed Himself to mankind in His word. His revelation is exclusive in both Testaments: "I am the LORD your God, who brought you out of the land of Egypt, out of the house of bondage. *You shall have no other gods before Me*" (Exod. 20:2-3). Paul wrote, "Therefore concerning the eating of things offered to idols, we know that an idol is nothing in the world, and that there is no other God but one. For even if there are so-called gods, whether in heaven or on earth (as there are many gods and many lords), yet for us there is one God, the Father, of whom are all things, and we for Him; and one Lord Jesus Christ, through whom are all things, and through whom we live" (1 Cor. 8:4-6).

God's will is revealed to mankind in His word, the Bible. The content of faith is defined by what is revealed in the Bible. One's personal faith is determined by his adherence to or rejection of that which is revealed in God's word. John wrote, "We are of God. He who knows God hears us; he who is not of God does not hear us. By this we know the spirit of truth and the spirit of error" (1 John 4:6). Consider these other verses:

> To the law and to the testimony! If they do not speak according to this word, it is because there is no light in them (Isa. 8:20).

> He who is of God hears God's words; therefore you do not hear, because you are not of God (John 8:47).

> My sheep hear My voice, and I know them, and they follow Me (John 10:27).

> If anyone thinks himself to be a prophet or spiritual, let him acknowledge that the things which I write to you are the commandments of the Lord (1 Cor. 14:37).

The faith that saves is a faith that takes God at His word and does what He says. A faith that chooses to commit itself to human wisdom, scientific theories, philosophical theories, and popular opinion over what is revealed in God's word has no power to save, regardless of how devoted one may be to that system of thought and how sincerely he might follow it. Many of the doctrines preached in the thousands of different twenty-first century churches are incompatible with and contrary to what is revealed in Scripture. They are like the "damnable heresies" introduced in first century churches (2 Pet. 2:1), damnable in the sense that they deny what is revealed by the Christ who bought them, lead men into lascivious conduct, and are taught by presumptuous men who have no restraint in railing against the revealed will of the Lord.

There are many questions one may ask a person to learn whether or not he has commitment to Jehovah, Jesus, and His word. Do you believe the world was created by the spoken word of God (Gen. 1; Psa. 33:6)? Do you believe that Jesus walked on water, fed 5000 with five loaves and two fish, and raised Lazarus from the dead? Do you believe that God separated the waters of the Red Sea to deliver His people from Egyptian bondage? Do you believe that God caused the sun to stand still so that Joshua could win the victory at Gibeon (Josh. 10:12)? Do you believe there was a Philistine warrior in Israel's battle with Gath who had six fingers on each hand and six toes on each foot (2 Sam. 21:20)? The issue is not how many toes the Philistine had, but do you commit yourself to following God's word. That is the issue being tested in all of these questions.

I was baptized at twelve years old and knew relatively little about the Bible at the time I was baptized. What I did understand and still understand is this: If someone can show me something from the Bible that I should believe and/or do that I am not presently believing or doing, my obligation is to start believing and/or doing it. If someone can show me something from the Bible that I am presently believing or doing that God does not want me to be believing or doing, my obligation is to stop believing and/or doing it. Why? Because my faith is in the God who revealed Himself in His word, not in the mere act of believing.

MIKE WILLIS